# HIDDEN SECRETS OF THE ROYAL MILE

A Self-guided Tour of Edinburgh's
Most Popular Tourist Site

Charron Moczygemba

ISBN: 979-8-9902348-0-2

# Dedication

This book is dedicated to my husband, who encouraged me; my daughter, who dared me; my eldest daughter, who listened to me; and to my two boys, who put up with me. I also want to dedicate this book to L.A. Blackburn, who mentored me; Shoshanna Grochowski, who edited for me; and Ariana Moczygemba, who designed the book cover for me. Thank you for all your support.

# Contents

Dedication ................................................................ 6

Introduction .............................................................. 12

Edinburgh Castle ...................................................... 14

Historical Objects within the Castle ............................. 4

Mary Queen of Scot's Tapestry ................................... 6

Laird's Lug ............................................................... 7

Statues and Memorials: Castle Esplanade ..................... 8

Robert the Bruce and William Wallace ......................... 18

Edinburgh Royal Mile ................................................ 22

Witches Memorial ...................................................... 25

Canonball Inn ............................................................ 29

Camera Obscura ......................................................... 31

Highland Tolbooth Kirk ............................................... 36

Riddler's Court ........................................................... 38

Deacon Brodie ............................................................ 42

Walter Francis Montagu: 5th Duke of Buccleuch, 7th Duke of Queensbury ............................................................. 47

St. Giles Cathedral ..................................................... 54

Mercat Cross ............................................................. 71

Old Tolbooth Prison .................................................... 77

Heart of Midlothian ..................................................... 81

David Hume Statue ..................................................... 83

Well Heads .................................................................. 86

Grassmarket .............................................................. 89

King Charles II Statue .............................................. 91

James Braidwood ..................................................... 95

Adam Smith ............................................................. 99

Statue Cones ........................................................... 102

Mary King's Close .................................................. 104

The Vault ............................................................... 108

Alexander & Bucephalus Statue ............................ 111

The Tron Kirk ........................................................ 114

Lady Stair's Close & Writer's Museum ................. 117

Gladstone's Land ................................................... 122

Paisley Close ......................................................... 127

John Knox House ................................................... 129

Tweeddale Court .................................................... 134

World's End ........................................................... 137

Netherbow Gate ..................................................... 139

Blue Police Box ..................................................... 141

Moray House - 1843 .............................................. 145

Canongate Kirk: 1649, 1688 ................................. 151

Canongate Tolbooth Tavern- 1591 ....................... 153

People's Story Museum .......................................... 157

Canongate Mercat Cross ........................................ 159

Queensberry House 1667 and 1808 ....................... 160

New Scottish Parliament ........................................... 164

Abbey Sanctuary .................................................... 166

Holyrood Palace ..................................................... 168

Lesser-Known Statues .............................................. 174

Greyfriars Bobby Statue ........................................... 180

1st Duke Wellington ................................................ 184

Calton Hill .......................................................... 186

Old Calton Cemetery ............................................... 193

Edinburgh Center Bollard .......................................... 196

Edinburgh's Dungeon ............................................... 198

Physics Garden ..................................................... 200

Unique Places to Visit ............................................. 203

Cows at Cowgate .................................................... 205

St. Culbert Kirkyard ................................................ 207

The Georgian House ................................................ 210

Miniature Lighthouse ............................................... 214

Princes Street Gardens ............................................. 218

Historical Monuments .............................................. 226

in Edinburgh ....................................................... 226

Arthur's Seat ....................................................... 236

St. Catherine's Well – Balms Well ................................ 239

Muschats Cairn ..................................................... 243

Only in Scotland ................................................... 246

Window Tax 1748 ............................................... 247

Edinburgh's Closes, ............................................. 249

Wynds, and Courts ............................................. 249

Endnotes ............................................................ 253

# Introduction

Walking down the Royal Mile in Edinburgh, Scotland, is like walking through a thousand years of history. Learn about the powerful tales and discover the hidden mystery of the medieval-modern city by peering behind the scenes to uncover secrets that are waiting to be shared to those who come. The Hidden Secrets of the Royal Mile brings to light the city's ancient past and its transformation into the modern world. Discover the meaning behind the Heart of Midlothian, and the time-honored tradition of spitting on the heart, the hidden tale about the strange ears on the Bucephalus statue, and the infamous 'Big Toe' of David Hume's statue. These are just a few of the many hidden stories surrounding the Royal Mile. This book offers readers the opportunity to not only walk through the city and admire all the historic buildings and statues along the way, but also provides understanding behind the places seen. By the time you finish reading through this book, you will have gained a deeper appreciation of all the hidden gems among Edinburgh's most popular tourist sites.

# Edinburgh Castle

i

$$\boxed{\text{\$\$\$ admission}}\qquad\boxed{\begin{array}{c}\text{Castle Hill, Royal Mile,}\\ \text{EH1 2ND, UK}\end{array}}$$

The famed Edinburgh Castle, which marks the beginning of the Royal Mile, has as much historic significance as the Old Town of Edinburgh, dating back to 1103. Known as Castle Rock, Edinburgh Castle was built on the rocky hillside of an extinct volcanic plug.[ii] The castle has been through many wars and sieges, giving Edinburgh Castle the title of the most besieged castle in Britain. Dating back to its early construction in the 10th century, Edinburgh Castle was under the control of Anglo-Saxon and Danish law; but for most of the history, the castle resided under the control of the British Crown. The strategic location of the castle made it a desirable place for invading forces. Furthermore, the location of the castle provided an excellent tactical position for the city to mount a defense against enemies seeking to overtake the city. Located along the border of the Lowlands of Scotland, this site became the center of the conflict between Scotland and England. Compounding the conflict between the two nations was an internal divide between the Lowlanders and the Highlanders. The Lowlanders were loyal to the British, while the Highland Jacobites rebelled against the English Crown. The castle had become embodied in the thickest of the conflict between the two warring nations during the Scottish War of Independence.

The ancient castle of Edinburgh is like a time capsule containing the history of the city. From early construction to modern times, the castle's buildings from different periods in its timeline have been preserved. One of the oldest buildings within the courtyards is Saint Margaret's Chapel. The chapel dates to 1130 and was built in honor of Queen Margaret, mother of King David I.

St. Margaret's Chapel is one of the most sacred buildings in Scotland. During the Scottish War of Independence in 1314, Robert the Bruce destroyed Edinburgh Castle, to prevent the English from occupying it, but spared St. Margaret's Chapel. Within St. Margaret's chapel, is a facsimile of the gospel book that Margaret brought with her to the castle. It is said that the book survived being dropped in the river and was retrieved without damage. Although the chapel no longer holds weekly services, it remains an active part of the city of Edinburgh as a place where weddings and Catholic christenings are celebrated.

## Evolution of St, Margaret's Chapel

- King David built the chapel in 1130.
- He dedicated the small building to his saintly mother.
- During the Protestant Reformation in 1560, the chapel was used as a gunpowder store, and its place in history was forgotten.
- In 1845, the original chapel was rediscovered. Queen Victoria had the chapel restored in 1881-1882.
- In 1922, stain-glass was added depicting Scotland saints and hero. St. Margaret, St. Columba, William Wallace, St. Andrew, and St. Ninan.

The history of sieges shaped the castle over the centuries,[iii] and frequently changed hands between the two countries. Over the years, the castle's defenses evolved, and several notable weapons of war gained fame. Mons Meg, known as one of the greatest medieval cannons ever created, was gifted to King James II in 1457. During the 1500s, when the castle fell under the control of the Scots, King James IV had the royal court moved to Edinburgh. The city became a proxy capital of Scotland in 1511, but the castle did not remain in Scottish hands very long when, in 1513, The Battle of Flodden[iv] took place and James IV had perished in the battle. The castle fell once again into English hands under King Henry VIII of England.[v] Under English rule, remarkable weapons were elevated to be distinctly identified for their success in changing the tides of battle. During the Lang Siege of 1573, bronze guns known as the 'Seven Sisters' were renowned for their role in keeping the enemy at bay.

By the early part of the 1600s, Edinburgh Castle began to experience a season of peace. Prior to the 17th century, Scotland and England existed as two nations, but upon the death of Queen Elizabeth I (she had no direct heir), the crown passed to the next heir in line, James VI, King of Scotland. King James VI represented both the Scottish Royal lines and the English Royalty. This established the unity of the monarchy for both England and Scotland, known as the Union of the Crowns.

Although Edinburgh Castle was under the English Crown, very little attention was paid to the castle since the English Crown preferred to remain in England instead of Scotland. This interlude of peace lasted until the 1650s, when Scottish Highlanders began the Jacobite uprising against the English Monarchy (1689-1745). Once again, the location was key for the English to use the castle as a military base. The castle's defenses were expanded with the addition of Dury's Battery and the Queen Anne building, which was constructed to house the soldiers and officers. Further expansion was added later during the Napoleonic Wars to house 600 soldiers stationed at the castle. The military history of the castle did not die away; rather, Edinburgh Castle is still used as an active military facility today.

# Historical Objects within the Castle

vi

The world's most famous medieval weapon, Mons Meg, provided the strength and authority of Scotland's kings. In 1449, Philip the Good ordered the construction of the giant cannon in Mons, Belgium to be given to King James II as a gift. In 1454, the wrought iron cannon was completed. The six-ton siege gun, capable of firing 150 kg gun stone over two miles, was the ideal cannon for Edinburgh Castle. Challenges arose in how to transport the enormous cannon from Belgium to Scotland. Her mass alone buckled most forms of transport. Before her, laboring workers leveled the route. Special carts were constructed requiring horses and oxen to drag the massive cannon overland to its destination. She barely traveled nine miles (14.5 km) a day.

In 1460, King James II employed Mons Meg in the siege of Roxburgh Castle, which required him to haul the cannon 50 miles away. Oxen were used to move the cannon three miles a day, roughly 16 days, until Mons Meg was deployed into action. Unfortunately, King James II was accidently killed when one of his other cannons exploded during the siege.

In 1495, King James IV hauled Mons Meg to Dunbarton Castle, and Northam Castle. By 1550, Mons Meg began showing her wear, and King James V's navy retired her. But her days of firing would once again be called into action when she was fired in the celebration of Mary Queen of Scots marriage in 1558. By 1681, Mons Megs firing days ended when her barrel exploded, and she was forced into eternal retirement. Today, visitors can see the famous siege cannon in its dormant state, residing in Edinburgh Castle once again,

# Mary Queen of Scot's Tapestry

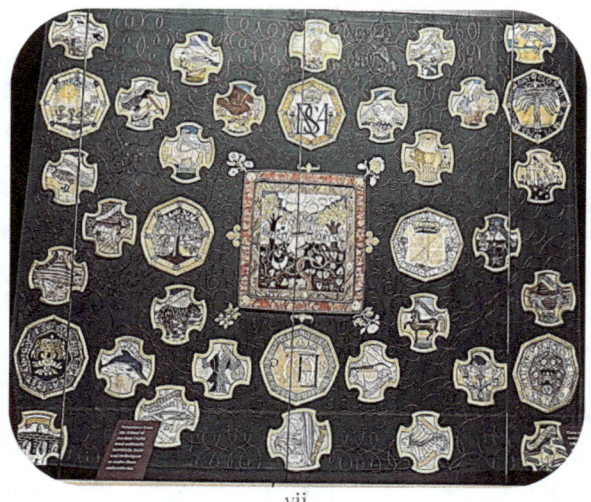

vii

In 1568, Mary Queen of Scot (Catholic) was forced to abdicate her throne to her two-year-old son James VI and leave him behind as she fled the country. She had petitioned her cousin Queen Elizabeth I (Protestant) for sanctuary. Queen Elizabeth I, fearing treachery from her cousin, consented for her to seek shelter in England, but kept her prisoner during her stay.

During Mary's long imprisonment of 18 and a half years, she used her time to hand sew these beautiful embroidery patches. Though none remain in good condition, efforts have been made to replicate Mary's original work.

# Laird's Lug

viii

Hidden away in the upper right-hand corner of the fire-place is a hidden window. The black gridles is known as the laird's lug, 'lord's ear'. Often taken for a vent, the lug was a tiny spy window that King James IV would use to spy on his guest below.

# Statues and Memorials: Castle Esplanade

ix

His Royal Highness the Field Marshal Frederick, Duke of York, and Albany, K.G., the British Army's MDCCXXVIL Commander in Chief August 16, 1763, born; January 5, 1827, died. He is George III's second son and George IV's brother. During the French Revolutionary Wars, he led two disastrous campaigns as field commander.

x

Edinburgh Castle Esplanade Scottish Horse Memorial Cross-The memorial is dedicated to the Scottish Horse Regiment who died in their call of duty in the South African War (1901-1902).

xi

## The Runic Cross

The Runic Cross was put on display for the public in 1862 in honor of the non-commissioned officers, and private soldiers assigned to the 78th Highland Regiment who died in the line of service during the First Relief of Lucknow in 1857 and during the Mutiny in 1857-1859. The Victoria Cross was awarded to the regiment.

## Gordon Highlanders

The memorial dedicated to the men of the Gordon Highlanders, who sacrificed their lives in battle during the South African War 1899-1902 in Natal, Transvaal, Cape Colony, and the Orange Free State. The regiment did not have a number assigned to them, rather they decided to take the name from Clan Gordon, where they were recruited from Aberdeen, Scotland.

xii

### 72nd Highlander Regiment Obelisk

A memorial to all military men under The Duke of Albany's 72nd Highlander regiment. The memorial honors the men who had made the ultimate sacrifice during the Afghan Campaigns: 1878, 1879, and in 1880.

xiii

## The 78th Highlanders Memorial Celtic Cross

The Celtic Cross was designed in memory of Col. Kenneth Douglas Mackenzie, who served Highlanders Regiment for 42 years. He died, while on duty in 1873.

XIV

### The Princess Louise's Argyllshire Highlander Fountain:

Princess Louise, Her Royal Highness, Marchioness of Lorne, 9th Duchess of Argyll, and Queen Victoria's daughter, had many honors given to her. The 91st Argyllshire had their name altered to the 91st Princess Louise's Argyllshire Highlander Regiment.

xv

## Ensign Ewart Memorial: Battle at Waterloo 1815 – (inscribed on the memorial)

"As Ewart fought his way deep into the heart of the 45th French Infantry, he was caught in a fierce fight with a French officer. The French officer was saved from Ewart's fatal strike by the arrival of Ewart's senior officer, Francis Kinchant. The French officer surrender to Kinchant thus saving his life. No sooner had Ewart turned away from the scene than he heard a gunshot just behind him. When he turned back, he saw senior officer Kinchant fall off his horse and the French Officer trying to hide his gun, which he [used to] ... kill[ed] Kinchant. Ewart, furious at the French Officer, pulled out his sword, ignoring the Frenchman's pleas for mercy, and took the Frenchman's head off with one stroke of his sword. (Sword located within the castle) Ewart was now near to the 45th French infantry standard bearer. Instead of retreating, Ewart continued forward and battled through to take the flag back to his own lines and into history" He passed at age 77 on March 23, 1846.

14

xvi

**Dean Ramsay** (1793-1872) was minister of St. John's in 1830. By 1841 he became the Dean. He is known for his ministry, philanthropy and his popular book, *Scottish Life and Reminiscences.* The Memorial displays Christ Resurrection and Ascension and acts of charity illustrated along the side panels combined with Celtic symbols.

xvii

**English (inscribed on the plaque):** "Hereabouts on the 19th of March in 1689 David Leslie, Earl of Leven, raised a Regiment of Foot in the space of two hours for the defense of the city. To commemorate this act and also the gallant behaviour of the new Regiment at the Battle of Killiecrankie some months later, the City Magistrates conferred upon LEVEN'S Regiment the unique right of recruiting by beat of drum in the City and of marching through the City at any time with drums beating, colours flying and bayonets fixed: the Regiment, later titled the 25th Edinburgh Regiment of Foot, is now known as THE KING'S OWN SCOTTISH BORDERERS and frequently exercises this privilege."

### Interesting fact:
if you look above the door you can see the initials MAH etched in the wood. The initials are from Mary Queen of Scot and her husband Henry Stewart. She gave birth to James VI who would later be king at 13 months old.

### Interesting facts:
The oldest crown jewels made during the reign of James IV and James V were first used in the coronation of Mary Queen of Scots in 1543.

xviii

17

# Robert the Bruce and William Wallace

xix

*(left side) Robert the Bruce & (right side) William Wallace Statue*

| $$$ admission | Castle Hill, Royal Mile, EH1 2ND, UK |
|---|---|

Edinburgh, Scotland, is a city where time seems to be frozen within the modern 21st century. Walking through the Royal Mile is like entering a time machine capturing over 1,000 years of Scottish history. The city exudes history from the buildings to the statues to the plaques, yet the Royal Mile still manages to represent modernization. At one end of the mile is Holyrood Palace, and at the other end stands Edinburgh Castle.

One of the most majestic and deeply entrenched icons of the Royal Mile is Edinburgh Castle. Over 1,000 years have passed since the castle's creation, and it remains intact today. Two statues of men frame the entrance. On the right is the statue of William Wallace and to the left is Robert the Bruce. The two famous men shaped Scotland's history and are celebrated as historic heroes. At first glance, the two statues would appear to be as old as the castle, but these famed statues are quite young in comparison, being added to the entrance in 1929. [xx/xxi/xxii]

William Wallace, a central leader in the 1st War of Scottish Independence. He raised an army against the British King Edward I. The Battle of Stirling Bridge (1297) marked the beginning of many battles he led in breaking the English control of Scotland. The English Crown succeeded in capturing Wallace in 1305 where he was executed. Robert the Bruce, a central leader in the War for Scottish Independence. He proclaimed himself King of Scotland in 1306. Like William Wallace, Robert the Bruce fought fearlessly for the Scottish people to regain their independence from the British Crown. Years of victorious battles and persistent resistance eventually broke the yoke of English control and by 1328 the Treaty of Edinburgh was signed in Northampton. The treaty officially recognized Scotland's Independence until King Bruce's death on June 7, 1329.

Both men represent the identity of the Scots and their strong history of resistance against the British Crown. On May 24, 1995, the film Braveheart portrayed Scotland's fight to free itself from the English Crown, bringing heroes from the past to life. While the movie version holds many truths, not everything that was depicted in the movie was accurate to the real history of the men who fought for Scotland's freedom.

**Interesting Fact:**
There is no historic record of either William Wallace or Robert the Bruce ever visiting Edinburgh Castle, and yet these two famous men have greeted visitors at the Castle's entrance since 1929.

**Interesting Fact:**
Robert the Bruce led his men to fight in the Battle of Bannockburn in 1314, winning victory over the English. He was considered King of Scotland when the Declaration of Arbroath was written in 1320.

**Interesting Fact:**
Author Randall Wallace, ancestor of William Wallace was inspired to research William Wallace's legacy. Randall's research eventually led to him writing a book that was later transformed into the movie 'Braveheart.'

**Interesting Fact:**
After Bruce's death his body was placed at Dunfermline Abbey in Fife, but his heart was preserved and was taken into battle and on crusades to be a symbol of Scotland. His heart was later buried in Melrose Abbey.

xxiii

# Edinburgh Royal Mile

xxiv<sub></sub>

xxiv

Edinburgh, Scotland, is in the lowlands near the border with England. Today, Edinburgh is the capital of Scotland, but this was not always the case. Originally, Scotland had another capital in Scone, near Perth. Scone was the official capital of Scotland in the 9th century and housed the Scottish Parliament in 1235. The capital moved to Edinburgh in 1437, after King James I, of Scotland, was murdered by an assassin. By 1452, Edinburgh had officially become the capital of Scotland.

The name Edinburgh ("burgh," defined as "fortress" or "walled collection of buildings")[xxv] is believed to have originated from the old English meaning 'Edwin's Fort' during the 7th century. [xxvi] The city of Edinburgh was also commonly known as "Auld Reekie." The Scottish term 'Auld Reekie' is roughly translated to mean "Old Smokey" referring to the pollution created by the burning of coal and wood fires, which would leave dark sooty marks along the chimneys and pollute the skies over the town. In medieval times, streets were designed on a slope and grooved in the center creating a funnel, so waste would accumulate and drain down to the local river below after it rained. For the city of Edinburgh, the Nor' Loch, in the northern part of the city, was where the toxic waste was drained from the streets.

The city of Edinburgh was facing many challenges during the 15th and 17th century: sanitation, population growth, limited expansion options, and waste management issues. As Edinburgh grew, the city struggled with housing the people moving into town. City expansion was limited by the capacity of the Flodden Walls surrounding the city. No one desired to leave the protection of the city gates for fear of potential invaders from outside. The solution was to keep the city within the boundaries of the Flodden Wall and keep up with the increased population during the 15th and 17th century by building the city upward. [xxvii] Soon, buildings grew from two stories high to 10 and 11 stories, causing Edinburgh to be one of the earliest skyscraper cities in the world.

Building skyscraper homes solved the population issue but created additional problems for the city. The lack of modern-day indoor plumbing limited how the population removed waste, and with added floors housing multiple families, the accumulation of waste removal soon flooded the streets in filth below. In time, these issues became a crisis that exceeded the city's ability to handle. The visible pollution and lack of indoor plumbing gave the town a repugnant odor that engulfed the streets of Edinburgh. In time, fortunately, sanitary technology was brought to the town, and the smell and poor sanitation conditions would disappear.

The only reminder of "Auld Reekie" is left in the faint memory of the same streets that mark the Old Town of days gone by, commonly known today as the Royal Mile.

## Interesting fact:

During the 15th to 17th century, it was common practice to throw waste and trash out the window onto the streets below. During this period in history people would shout out 'gardy-loo' as they deposited their waste from the window to land below. The call out would warn people passing beneath the window to step clear of the contents being thrown down below. This unpleasant action would later translate into the bathroom being called the 'loo' referring to the 17th century sanitation removal method.

## Best Castle Photo Locations:

- The Vennel
- St. Cuthbert's Churchyard
- Rose Fountain - Princes Street Gardens
- Castle Esplanade
- Roof Terrace at National Museum of Scotland
- Salisbury Craig

# Witches Memorial

xxviii/xxix

Castle Hill, Royal Mile, EH1
2ND, UK

The Witch's Well Memorial is one of Edinburgh's smallest monuments, highlighting a very dark period in Edinburgh's history between the 16th to 18th centuries. The monument is often overlooked by visitors lured away by the magnificent Edinburgh Castle looming at the top of the ancient volcano. Located on the eastern corner of the Edinburgh Castle Esplanade, the site of the Witch's Well Memorial was originally used as a reservoir that held the town's water supply.

The story behind the fountain memorial dates to

the 16th century. Women who were suspected of being witches [xxx] were sent to trial and endured tests to prove that they weren't witches. The problem with the tests was that the accused were often the casualties of the witches' tests. Anyone who survived was then declared a witch, but if a person died in the process of the test, the individual was declared innocent. It is estimated that a total of 4,000 people, mainly women, were accused of being witches, died in front of Edinburgh Castle. By the end of the 17th century, witches were routinely hung instead of burning at the stake. The last hanging took place in 1728.

Like the Salem Witch Trials in Massachusetts, the witch scare cost many innocent women and men their lives. The witch trials are traced back to King James VI's Great Scottish Witch Hunt. He strongly believed that witchcraft was abundant in his kingdom and declared war against anyone suspected of acting in concert with the devil. When a person was accused of witchcraft, they were dragged from their homes and put on display before the town. The Witch Trial hearings took place at the local church, where evidence was gathered and presented to the High Court.

The Witch Trials were merely ritualistic acts performed in front of an audience. Most of the evidence against the person was circumstantial and based on very few facts. Examples of evidence include having red hair, a mole on a particular spot on a person's body, a person seen walking around late in the night, an individual who did not fit in well with others, and a person who may have had a vendetta against a neighbor. During the hearing process, heinous methods were used to force the accused to confess to their crime of witchcraft. These methods of torture included forced sleep deprivation, body mutilation, water dunking, and water floating. If the defendant failed to confess, a final test to garner absolute proof was necessary. The accused was thrown into the Nor Loch (now Princes Street Gardens) with her left hand or thumb tied to her right foot and her right hand and thumb tied to her left foot, leaving little hope of floating or treading water. If the accused sank, they were declared innocent, a rope tied around her middle-prevented drowning." [xxxi] If the victim floated, then her fate was sealed, and she was hung, followed by the body being burned afterward. Historically, the most heinous sentence for a person accused of witchcraft took place on June 25, 1519. Dame Euphane MaCallan was blamed for casting a spell that demolished King James VI's ship as it was porting at North Berwick. The High Court declared she was a witch, and she was sentenced to be "bound to a stake and burned in ashes, quick to the death." [xxxii]

A significant number of people condemned for witchcraft gave Scotland the nickname of being the biggest prosecutor in Europe. A sad title to earn. By the end of the 17th century, witches were routinely hung instead of burned. The last hanging took place in 1728.

The small witch memorial displays artistic symbolism on the plaque near the three-sided trough. The front image depicts flora and roots representing the earth and branches above. Additional images on the left side are an evil eye with both eye and nose frowning. Under the eye are words inscribed, "the evil eye." On the right side are hands holding a bowl with the inscription "hand of healing" below.

The memorial was designed by John Duncan in 1894, commissioned by Sir Patrick Geddes. He created the drinking fountain, on the west side of Castlehill Reservoir, next to Ramsey Garden. On the plaque, a small trough sticks out to hold water, and the image above is of foxglove plants with a snake coiled around the head of Aesculapius, caduceus, a medical symbol of the god of medicine and his daughter Hygeia, the goddess of health. The foxglove plant symbolizes the medical use of the plant, but foxglove is poisonous depending on the dosage given. The snake image symbolizes wisdom and represents good and evil. When the fountain runs, water is seen coming out of the snake's head, like a spout. Above the left corner of the plaque, one can find Roman numerals 1479 and 1722. The dates on the monument represents the Witch trials that had taken place in the city. On the lower left of the plaque, the artist's initials can be found next to the memorial's date of commission, 1894.

Today, tourists can see this memorial, which now holds flowers instead of water. The Witches Well is cared for by a local woman who takes time to water the flowers in the trough. People who notice the small fountain sometimes leave cards at the site in remembrance of those who died during the dark time in the city of Edinburgh, Scotland.

# Canonball Inn

xxxiii

*Canon ball on the Inn Wall*

356 Castlehill, Royal Mile,
EH1 2ND, UK

Often overlooked by many visitors and locals, Cannon-ball Inn holds within its walls a mystery that has not been answered. The mystery of the Cannonball Inn is described in its name. On the outside of the wall, as you walk from Castle Esplanade to Castle Hill, embed-ded between the 2nd and 3rd window is a cannonball. No one knows how or when the cannonball appeared in the wall or when it happened. One theory suggests that the mysterious cannonball was fired from Edinburgh Castle toward Holyrood Palace in 1745. During this period, the 3rd Jacobite Rising took place, and Bonnie Prince Charlie had been residing at the location with

29

his Jacobite advisors. Many locals dismiss this story as being inaccurate. A second, less thrilling, theory is that the cannonball was purposely placed on the building by a local engineer as a water level marker to indicate the exact height of the spring at Comiston. The spring was located seven miles away in the south and provided the water supply for the town in 1621. No one knows for certain why the cannonball is in the wall, but one thing is certain: it stirred the imagination of people who spotted the small cannonball on the wall of Cannonball Inn.

# Camera Obscura

xxxiv

$$$ admission | 549 Castle Hill, Royal Mile, EH1 2ND, UK

Along the Royal Mile, near Castle Hill, is a rather unusual building called the Camera Obscura. Atop the building is a white dome-like structure housing an interesting piece of history and scientific illusions. Although this building is not the original location of the Camera Obscura, the mysterious story is quite interesting to tell.

Thomas Short, a skilled optician from Leith, created the first great refracting telescope during the 18th century. Together, he and his brother, James

31

Short, brought the 12-foot-long telescope and other scientific instruments to Edinburgh, forming the first observatory on Calton Hill in 1776. [xxxv] The brothers planned to charge a small entrance fee to provide the public with the opportunity to witness the latest scientific tools and look through the refracted telescope. Short had benefited from a grant provided by Colin Maclaurin, the professor of mathematics at Edinburgh University. The grant provided a lease for one acre of land on Calton Hill for 99 years and financial funding for the Observatory for 35 years. The only stipulation required Short to offer the university students access to the telescope.

xxxvi

Thomas Short commissioned architects James Craig and Robert Adams to draw up plans for the observatory located in New Town. Short's original instruction for the building was an octagonal tower that stood 48 feet high and housed an east and west pavilion. Robert Adams convinced Short to design the building to resemble a fortress with embrasures and buttresses. The plans changed once more when the town council lost interest in funding the cost of completing the project. In the end, the Grand Fortress Observatory design was significantly scaled back. [xxxvii]

By 1788, Thomas Short had passed away, and the Observatory was willed to his grandson, James Douglas, who attempted to fulfill his grandfather's plan. Douglas charged 2 shillings to visit the observatory. Internal family conflict soon ended Thomas Short's dream for the public observatory when Short's wife protested the will and demanded her rightful ownership of the telescope. One night she managed to sneak into the observatory and steal the telescopes, refracting mirrors, and additional items she believed were her own. In retribution against Short's wife, Douglas was forced to issue a warrant to get the refracted mirrors back.

Widow Short did not take kindly to being kicked out of her home, and she returned to the observatory fully armed with a pistol, cutlasses, and blunderbuss. [xxxviii] The Town Guards were called to disrupt Ms. Short's plans for an armed takeover, and she was arrested and locked away. As for James Douglas, the Observatory failed to secure his financial needs. He closed the observatory and went back to work at sea.

Over time, the Observatory was purchased and sold as various businesses but never could sustain itself. The observatory was ignored, and time took its toll on the building and the equipment. Thomas Short's dream of having a functioning observatory had failed.

By 1807, the former observatory had become a gunpowder store open to the public. In 1827, Maria Theresa Short returned to Edinburgh from the West Indies and laid claim to the observatory. She claimed to be the only existing daughter of Thomas Short. Maria Short soon realized she had no claims to the observatory, which, by this time, was solely in the hands of the Edinburgh Astronomical Institution. Like her mother, Maria did not let this stop her from claiming her rightful ownership of the telescope. In protest, she asserted that she had aided her father in the telescope project and, by right, should have ownership of the work she contributed to her father's design. Her claims provided her with ownership of the great telescope in 1835, and she was allowed to build a wooden structure to mount the telescope near the national monument. [xxxix]

The story of the observatory does not end with Maria being given her father's telescope. Additional controversy followed. The observatory promoted the use of three powerful telescopes in addition to the Camera Obscura and other scientific instruments. The opposition claimed that the telescopes were not as advanced as they were advertised to be. Furthermore, the public began complaining about people with ill intentions who were using the Observatory as a peep show, using the telescope as a tool to view people or things they shouldn't. Protests at the observatory eventually prompted the town council to remove the telescopes and Camera Obscura from the site. After the town council ordered the closure of Camera Obscura, over 4,000 people signed a petition against the removal, but the signatures did not prove to be enough for the council to revoke the order. By 1850, Maria was forced to leave the premises.

With a firm belief in continuing the Observatory, Maria Short relocated the Observatory to Edinburgh Castle Hill and opened the facility to the public once again with the addition of a museum of scientific curiosities. Today, the legacy of Thomas Short's famed refracted telescope and advances in scientific instruments have been fulfilled by his lost daughter from India. The Observatory was later taken over by urban planner Patrick Geddes, who had renamed the Observatory 'Outlook Tower'. Patrick Geddes took his passion for urban planning and added his own to the Outlook Tower by expanding the facility to encompass worldly exhibits. Today, Camera Obscura Outlook Tower has morphed into a scientific funhouse using lights, lasers, and perspective illusions to trick the brain.

# Highland Tolbooth Kirk

xl

Free admission

348 Castle Hill, Royal Mile,
EH1 2ND, UK

The Highland Tolbooth Kirk is an amazing Neo-Gothic building dating back to 1842. The Tolbooth Kirk is deceptive in its design, hinting at the building being much older than it seems. The Neo-Gothic design by Scottish architect James Gillespie Graham and English architect Augustus Pugin achieved this design by using dark sandstone in the building's construction. Spires that reach 72 feet in the sky make this unique building hard to miss as one walks along the Old Town on the Royal Mile.

The Tolbooth Kirk is not only misleading in its physical appearance. but also, in its name. In Scotland, the word kirk means church, indicating the Highlands Tolbooth Kirk was formerly a church. This is not the case. The kirk never operated as a church; rather, the Church of Scotland commissioned the building as a meeting place for the General Assembly. In 1929, the Church of Scotland relocated to a new Assembly Hall at the Mound. Over the next 50 years, Tolbooth Kirk was used by different congregations. In 1979, the congregations decided to unite at the Greyfriars' Kirk. The Tolbooth Kirk remained locked for the next twenty years. The doors were reopened in 1999 with a different name and purpose. The former Highland Tolbooth Kirk became the Hub, which has a redesigned interior and serves the city as a multifunctional building that ranges from a tourist information center to hosting international festivals. In addition, it served as a temporary parliament building assembly hall between 1999-2004 until the new Parliament building was completed. xli

# Riddler's Court

xlii

Free admission

322 Lawnmarket, Edinburgh,
EH1 2PG, UK

It is said that "Edinburgh is often described as being like the bones of a fish. The Royal Mile is the spine, and the bones are the Closes', including wynds and courts, or passageways on either side." [xliii] A close is a narrow lane or alleyway of Edinburgh's medieval past. The term close refers to the tight spaces between buildings. At one time, the city boasted of having 248 closes but over time, as buildings were torn down and modern elements were added, the closes began disappearing. Today, only 80 closes remain, in various conditions. Some are private to the public, and others are dead ends, but there are also some to explore and find hidden gems that are often overlooked. [xliv]

One particular close is called Riddle's Close, built in the 1590s. The Riddle's building is considered one of the oldest buildings on the Royal Mile. Bailie McMorran, a wealthy merchant, built the impressive residence. Five years later in 1595, McMorran was called to end a student riot taking place in the building. The incident happened on the town's public holiday, but the students at The Royal High School were denied the day off. In their anger, they decided to protest the unjust act of denying the students a day off. The students barricaded themselves in their rooms in Riddler's Court and refused to surrender or vacate the building. Soon the student protest escalated, and the town's militia was called to put an end to the students' actions. [xlv]

When the militia moved in, the students began to panic. One student had a loaded musket, took aim through the open window, and fired at the militia as they approached. The student's aim was true, and Bailie McMorran was shot and died. The student who fired the musket was the son of William Sinclair, a prominent member of society. Sinclair's influence succeeded in preventing any consequence from happening to his son, and no conviction was declared.

## Interesting theory:

The term 'Got off Scot Free' is believed to have originated with the student protest in 1595. The theory is based upon the student not being charged for the murder of Bailie McMorran.

After the student protest in 1595, the property changed hands and hosted many notable people over the years. King James VI attended the Royal Banquet in Riddler's Court in 1598. Scotland's famous philosopher, David Hume, once rented an apartment in the court in 1751. The name Riddler's Court was not the official name of the building; it was named after one of the building's later owners, George Riddler, in 1726.

Over the years, various changes were made to the building, and remodeling helped to maintain the residence. Like many buildings along the Royal Mile, the buildings were modified throughout the years to accommodate the changing world around them. During the city census in 1881, Riddler's Court was recorded to have housed 247 residents. The population in the building far exceeded the limits of the structure. The census provided a real-life account of the city's overpopulation problems and the decline of the Old Town. The building that had once been heralded for its beauty and hosted royal banquets, later became known as the city's slum building, was deemed too costly to save and set up for demolition.

Yet this would not be the end of the Riddler building. Patrick Geddes had a vision to bring life back to the historic structure. Geddes was a conservationist who believed in saving the history and architecture of the city. After purchasing the old building, Geddes began a 'root to branch' restoration. [xlvi] When the restoration was complete, the old Riddler building was transformed into the first Hall of Residence for the University of Edinburgh summer school in 1887. Inscribed on the gate entry is a Latin phrase, 'Vivendo Discimus', translated as 'By living, we learn'.[xlvii]

Today, Riddler Court is protected under the Edinburgh World Heritage Organization. The EWH works to save the buildings of Edinburgh's past in hopes of keeping the history of the city alive for future generations to see. Through extensive fundraising efforts, donations throughout the globe help fund restoration efforts to preserve the ancient structures.

Walking through Riddler's Court along the sides of the walls, are plaques displaying the significant history of Riddle's Court and the people who impacted the history of Edinburgh. Well-known people such as David Humes, Patrick Geddes, and King James VI are just a few people who played a major role in shaping the history of Edinburgh.

# Deacon Brodie

xlviii /xlix

*Deacon Brodie's Tavern*

$$$ Tavern

435 Lawnmarket, Edinburgh, EH1 2NT, UK

Robert Louis Stevenson was born and raised in Edinburgh, Scotland. Throughout his life, he, like many others, heard the story of William Brodie. William Brodie (1741-1788) was a skilled craftsman and had earned the respectable title of Deacon of the Incorporation of Wrights. The title gave Brodie certain liberties within the community, providing him a seat on the city council. He was also known for his skills as a locksmith and had acquired many customers with his vocation. Having earned a political position in the city and the title of Deacon of the Wright Corporation, Brodie was trusted with open access to wealthy client homes. Brodie could then attend his client's home and complete his work without anyone watching over him.

Brodie, in every sense of the word, had a successful career, a respectable reputation, and a nice family to come home to. What many people did not know was Brodie's darker side. William Brodie loved to drink and gamble. He also liked women. Over the years, he had two mistresses, giving him five illegitimate children to support. Soon, the heavy drinking, gambling debt, and financial obligations exceeded his earnings and inheritance. Desiring to continue his dual life, he decided to use a wax impression to create his own personal key to customers' homes. He would break into his clients' residences in the evenings, when they were out, to steal their hidden treasures. His clients had no idea of Brodie's sinister activities. Brodie, on the other hand, had found the solution to fund his darker life while maintaining his image as a trustworthy man the city of Edinburgh had known him to be. [1]

Brodie's double life quickly became too much for him to keep up with. His second solution was to hire three men to help in his theft ring: John Brown, George Smith, and Andrew Ainslie. Life was going well for Brodie, but things would quickly come to a crashing conclusion with all of Brodie's secrets revealed before the whole city. During one of the heists, Andrew Ainselie's robbery of the city's Excise Office in Chessle's Court failed. To avoid punishment, Ainslie promptly went to the local police, seeking a King's pardon for the crime. During the interrogation, Ainslie disclosed the whole operation, revealing everyone's names in his confession. [li]

William Brodie quickly fled the country and went to the Netherlands, but he was soon caught in Amsterdam and brought back for trial in Edinburgh. As the trial concluded, Brodie's double lives were aired before the citizens of Edinburgh. The verdict was guilty, and he was sentenced to death by hanging on October 1, 1788. Brodie was jailed at the Tolbooth Prison until his public hanging took place before 40,000 people. The story of William Brodie was one of shock and intrigue, and it stunned the people of Edinburgh.

lii

*William Brodie, Deacon of Wrights & Mason of Edinburgh was the son of a cabinet maker in the Lawnmarket. He was born in Brodie Close and hanged near St. Giles - both places being just a few steps from the tavern which now bears his*

44

*name. In Manhood, Brodies baseness inspired Robert Louis Ste-*
*venson to write that famous classic Dr. Jekyll & Mr. Hyde. By*
*day William Brodie was pious, wealthy, and much respected citi-*
*zen and in 1781 on elected Deacon Councillor of the city. But at*
*night he was a gambler, a thief, dissipated and licentious. The*
*annuals record His cunning and audacity were unsurpassed.*
*Brodie was hanged from the city's new gallows on Oct. 1, 1788.*
*Ironically, he had designed the gallows that were to eventually*
*seal his fate.*

William Brodie and his double life inspired
Robert Louis Stevenson, a famed author, to write the
story The Strange Case of Dr. Jekyll and Mr. Hyde.
The story is about a man living two lives. One life as a
well-respected man in society with a second persona
living a wildlife. Unlike William Brodie, Stevenson
used a chemical concoction to create a literal transformation in the case of Dr. Jekyll and Mr. Hyde. As
night transformed into day, so did Mr. Hyde into Dr.
Jekyll. The story ends this conflict between the two
personalities with the deaths of both. The similarities
between the real story of William Brodie and Stevenson's Dr. Jekyll and Mr. Hyde are uncanny. Today, the
story of William Brodie is not as commonly known as
Stevenson's version, but it lives on in Stevenson's story
of a real man who lived the life of a respectable citizen
by day and a life of darkness at night.

**Interesting fact:**
Brodie was commissioned by the City of Edinburgh to construct a more efficient design of a hangman's gallows. The design became the very structure which Brodie was hung from.

**Interesting fact:**
The name Mr. Hyde is a play on words meaning that Dr. Jekyll was seeking to hide his darker side from society.

**Interesting fact:**
Stevenson owned one of William Brodie's cabinets in his childhood room.

**Interesting Facts:**
Deacon Brodie Pub is named after the actual Deacon William Brodie criminal, while Deacon Brodie Close is named after Deacon Brodie's father.

# Walter Francis Montagu: 5th Duke of Buccleuch, 7th Duke of Queensbury

liii

High Street, Edinburgh,
EH1 1RE, UK

Located in front of St. Giles Cathedral, in the old Parliament Square, is an imposing statue of a man gazing upon the city. The statue is of Walter Francis Douglas

47

Scott, 5th Duke of Buccleuch and 7th Duke of Queensbury (1806-1884). The duke received his title at the
young age of 13, after the passing of his father. He in-
herited a wealth of land throughout Scotland and parts
of England. He gained his knighthood by 1835 and
served as a member of the Scottish Parliament (a con-
servative politician) in 1840 under Prime Minister Robert Peel.

The duke passed away in 1884, and by 1885,
the Edinburgh Council had designed a memorial to the
duke in Parliament Square. In Victorian Gothic fashion, the duke's statue wears the Robe of the Thistle,
which is the highest Order of Chivalry in Scotland. The
statue was finished in 1887, but when the duke's statue
was placed upon the three-tiered platform, the statue
was too large for the pedestal. Fortunately, with mod-
ifications, the original bronze decoration that had
adorned the top of the podium was removed. This provided a bit more space for the duke to be placed on the
pedestal.[liv] The completed statue was unveiled before
the public on February 7, 1888. The oversized statue
has a unique 3D effect, as if his foot is stepping off the
pedestal. The detailed engraved images depicted
throughout the statue testify to the importance and impact he had in the city. The statue has three tiers: the
first tier depicts the images of a huntsman and his
hounds chasing stags; the second tier displays images
of the duke's life. The third tier illustrates significant
moments in Scott's family life. At the corners of the
tier are four rampant stags holding the armorial shield.

# Second tier on the Duke's Statue

lv

- NE side - The Duke is the colonel in charge of his militia.
- SW side - The Duke is drawing up plans for Granton Harbour.
- NW - Duke receives Queen Victoria at Dalkeith on her 1st visit to Scotland in 1842.
- NW - depicts the families coat of arms.
- SE - illustrates the celebration of the duke's 70th birthday given by his tenantry in 1878.

- E - commemorates when the duke was given the title of Chancellor of Glasgow University.

# Third tier, base level, of the statue

lvi/lvii

lviii/
lix

## Panels and their description

- Sir Walter Scott's (4th Lord of Rankilburn & Murthockson) death in 1402 at the Battle of Homildon Hill.
- Meeting with Queen Elizabeth: Buccleuch arrived in London in 1596 to appease the Queen after he had attacked the Castle of Carlisle to rescue Kinmont Willie.

51

- The English burning of Catslack Tower in Yarrow in 1548, which caused the death of lady Buccleuch.
- Sir Walter Scott of Buccleuch attempted to rescue Branxholm of James 5th Earl of Angus in 1532.
- In 1532 the English burned Branxholme during their raid.
- The rise of the Scott clan, led by Warden Buccleuch, to attack the English in retaliation raid.

lx

Parliament Sq., Edin-
burgh, EH1 1RF, UK

**Significance dates:**

Located on the West of Parliamentary Square near the 5th Duke of Buccleuch are three dates inscribed on three bronze bricks on the ground. Each date is significant, representing an historic event in Scotland. 1386, marks the rebuilding of the St. Giles Church and the Tolbooth; after it was burnt down by Richard II. 1430, (October 16) is the year James I of

52

Scotland was born at Holyrood Palace. 1610 the Tolbooth was added to house the prisoners.

# St. Giles Cathedral

lxi

> Free admission

> High Street, Edinburgh, EH1 1RE, UK

The origin of St. Giles Cathedral is a bit hazy, with current knowledge comparable to vague memories. Although the building is traditionally believed to date back to 1124, some historians theorize that the age of the church, in its basic form, could date from as early as 824 A.D. Within this hypothesis, historians claim that the building may not have been officially dedicated as a church during ancient times. Historians have found records of the church dedicated by the Bishop of St. Andrews in 1243, and years later the church was renamed and rededicated as St. Giles.[lxii] Although this is not historically backed by evidence, many theorize that the church's rededication from the original name of St. Andrew to St. Giles (French saint) was a political move to unite the French and Scottish nations together. With many buildings surviving the test of time, St. Giles Cathedral serves as a reminder of the significant role the church played in shaping the world in the 21st century.

lxiii

The stone carving depicts St. Giles holding a Roe that had been shot with a deadly arrow.

lxiv

    To the left is Bishop William Forbes (1634) he was the first Bishop of Edinburgh. Sadly, he passed away on April 12, 1634, soon after he became the first Bishop.

On the right is Alexander Henderson he became the Presbyterian of St. Giles. In 1641, King Charles appointed him Dean of the Chapel Royal at Holyrood. Henderson was a key writer of the National Covenant. He passed away in 1646 and is buried in Greyfriars Churchyard.

lxv

Located above the west side of the door of St. Giles is the image of St. Andrew holding two fish. Beneath the statue the identity of the statue is displaying on the scroll, and above his head are two additional angels with St. Andrew Cross.

lxvi

(Below) King David I, known as the Scottish King, is recognized for his success in the battle of Largs (1263). He is attributed to ending the threat of the Norsen King Haakon IV from the West Isles. During his reign he also added the Isle of Man and Hebrides to Scottish land, upon the signing of the Treaty of Perth in 1266.

lxvii

King James I (center) was crowned king in Scone, Scotland in 1423, but was declared king after the passing of his father. The gap in his rule was due to him being imprisoned in the London jail for 17 yr. During his imprisonment, James I's uncle, Robert of Albany, ruled in his stead. At the age of 30, James I regained his freedom and his crown. He was later murdered in 1437 at the Dominican Monastery, Perth-shire Scotland.

To the left, is Robert the Bruce. He was crowned King of Scotland on March 25, 1306. The defeat of English King Edward II in the Battle of Bannockburn in June of 1314 re-established Scottish independence from England, reclaiming Sterling Castle. He passed on June 7, 1329, and was buried at Dunfermline Abbey and his heart is located at Melrose Abbey.

King James VI (Scotland) & I (England), son of Mary Queen of Scots and Henry Darnley. He was born in Edinburgh Castle in 1566. James VI/I am the youngest king ever to serve in Scotland at the age of 13 months old in 1603. He also became king of three kingdoms: Ireland, Scotland, and England. James VI/I passed away at 58 yrs. old in 1625 at Westminster Abbey.

lxviii /lxix

On the left is the statue of Gavin Douglas. He was born at Tantallon Castle, in Dunbar E. Lothian in 1474. Douglas wore many hats as: Bishop, at Dunkled-1516, royal court Poet, and provost of St. Giles in 1501. Although he had many roles, he is best known for his translations of Virgil's Aeneid into both the Scottish and English languages." He passed in London in 1522. On the right is the statue of John Knox who served as minister at St. Giles Church in 1560. He is known as

60

the 'Greatest Reformer in Scotland'. He passed on November 24, 1572, and is believed to have been buried in the St. Giles Parking lot #23.

lxx

To the left is King Alexander I born in 1078. He was the oldest of the three brothers. During his reign, he created the Augustinian priory located at Scone in 1122. The following year, Alexander I embarked on a journey to the Inchcolm Isles, Firth of Forth in the middle of a storm. Fearing for his life, he vowed that if he lived, he would build a monastery on the Isle, but sadly, he passed and could not fulfill his vow. His brother, King David I, fulfilled his brother's promise. Alexander I is buried at Stirling Castle on April 23, 1124, and is buried at Dunfermline Abbey.

Alexander III (right) became king at the young age of 7 years old in 1249. During his reign he is credited for adding the territory of the Isle of Man and the Western Isle of Scotland, which he obtained after the

61

passing of the Norwegian King Haakon. Within the Treaty of Perth, Norway still maintained control of Orkney and Shetland. Alexander III passed after a horse-riding accident at Kinghorn of Fife on March 18, 1286. He was on a journey to visit his wife for her birthday when he fell from his horse. He is buried with his brothers in Dunfermline Abbey. A monument was built at the place of his death in Kinghorn, Scotland.

*A wooden carved bagpipe angel is in the Thistle Chapel.*
lxxi

Within the Cathedral, in the Thistle Chapel, lie interesting wooden carvings of three angels playing bagpipes. Two of the angels (one above the right corner and one tucked in the corner across the entrance) are camouflaged within the detailed wood carvings. The last angel is composed of stone and is stationed to overlook the windows. The Three Bagpipe Angels are a favorite to see in the cathedral.

One of the most notable historical points worth mentioning is the church's close ties with the Scottish Reformation. Within the walls of the church, John Knox served as a minister for 13 years. During his time, Knox set in motion dynamic changes in reforming the religious view of the church. The Scottish Reformation was a movement to separate the church and state by breaking the papacy and instituting Calvinistic theology within the Church of Scotland. The new theology morphed into a heavily Presbyterian religious belief that grew beyond the borders of Scotland and spread throughout Europe during the 16th century.[lxxii]

### St. Giles Day

The traditional St. Giles' Day parade was also interrupted by Protestants trying to break images of Saints. On his return to Scotland in 1559, John Knox marched an army of followers into St. Giles' and preached there for the first time. The following week he was elected its minister, and the building was stripped of its Catholic decoration.

The Scottish Parliament abolished papal authority in 1560 and 400 years of St. Giles' as a Catholic church officially came to an end. Inside the building, the stained-glass windows were removed, and the icons were destroyed. This was despite Scotland still having a Catholic ruler, Mary Queen of Scots, who John Knox publicly denounced in his sermons.

By the time of Knox's death in 1572, whilst still a minister of St. Giles', Scotland was becoming a leading Protestant European nation. Despite many controversies and complications its Presbyterian system of church government, democratic tradition and commitment to education were becoming dominant with lasting consequences. John Knox and those he inspired were essential in this achievement.
lxxiii

John Knox, born around 1513 in Haddington, east Lothian, John Knox was the leading figure of the Scottish Reformation which led to the establishment of the Presbyterian form of the church governance of Scotland.

Knox originally trained as a Roman Catholic priest but joined a growing reformation movement in 1540's. After being caught up in ecclesiastical and political events at St. Andrews, he was taken prisoner and enslaved on a French galley ship. On his release he went into exile and eventually to Geneva, in Switzerland, where he befriended the French reformer John Calvin who greatly influenced Knox's understanding of the church. In 1558 Protestantism was beginning to take hold in Scotland. One night a statue of St. Giles was stolen from the church, which was still Catholic in practice, and thrown into Edinburgh's Nor' Loch, a putrid body of water that once filled Princes Street Gardens.

During 13 years of service, Knox's reform movement altered the role of St. Giles from a Catholic church into a community-centered church for the town. The transformation of religious beliefs occurred rather peacefully, without riots or protests. St. Giles was also redesigned to expand its role in the town to be used as a police station, school, fire station, coal store, and prison. In addition, over the years, the church has also served as a facility for the Scottish Parliament, town council, and General Assembly of the Church of Scotland. [lxxiv] St. Giles became deeply embedded within the history and function of the community it resided in. The infamous execution device, known as the Maiden Guillotine, was stored within the church (but is now located in the Scottish Museum).

**Interesting Fact:**
St. Giles is not really a Cathedral. Instead, the ancient building is a Kirk, which translate as 'church'. St. Giles is considered the High Kirk of Edinburgh.

lxxv

## Jenny Geddes

Following the 1603 Union of the Crowns, Scotland and England began to share the same monarch, though the two countries were still independent kingdoms for the next hundred years. In 1637 King Charles I attempted to draw the Scottish church, which was Presbyterian, into line with the English Church, which was Anglican. There was widespread public discontent that Scotland's independent church system, established by the Scottish Parliament in 1560, was being overridden by a king in London while little understanding of his northern kingdom.

Scottish opposition came to the boil when Charles I Prayer to impose a new Common Prayer in St. Giles. According to tradition a local women named Jenny Geddes picked up her stool and threw it at the preacher. Suddenly a riot erupted in the building and church services were suspended for a week for fear of public uprising.
lxxvi

lxxvii

*Jenny Geddes, throwing her stool, at Hannay, Dean of St. Giles*

By the 1600s, the Scottish Reformation had completely transformed the church and the Scottish people. King Charles I, a Catholic English king, sought to reign the Scottish Reformers back under the thumb of the English Crown. To achieve unity among the kingdoms, King Charles I and William Laud, Archbishop of Canterbury, decided to force all churches in Scotland to become Anglicans by instituting the New Anglican Prayer Book, also known as the Common Book of Prayer, in 1637. A copy of the prayer book was distributed to St. Giles by Scottish Episcopal bishops and Archbishop Laud. lxxviii The members of St. Giles were not pleased with the introduction of the Anglican prayer book.

The story takes place on July 23, 1637. James Hannay, Dean of St. Giles, used the required new Anglican prayer book in his service. Jenny Geddes, the local cabbage street vendor, became furious over the new prayer book being used in the church. In her rage, she stood up and grabbed her three-legged stool. She threw the stool at Dean Hannay's head, shouting, *"'De'il gie you colic, the wame o' ye, fause thief; daur ye say Mass in my lug?"* meaning loosely, *"Devil give you colic, false thief; dare you say the Mass in my ear?"* [lxxix] Jenny Geddes sparked others in the congregation to join in on her objection to the mandated prayer book. When the people ran out of stools and bibles to throw, they began yelling and shouting their protest. Even after being removed from the church, they beat at the doors and shattered the windows. The protestors quickly gathered the attention of other townspeople, who also joined in on the riot. The rioters encircled Edinburgh City Chambers, threatening a civil war.

King Charles I was steadfast in his determination not to yield to the rioters' demands. The Scottish rebels formed an organized resistance and created a National Covenant on February 28, 1638, in Greyfriars Churchyard in Edinburgh, Scotland. The covenant boldly "rejected the attempt by King Charles I and William Laud, Archbishop of Canterbury, to force the Scottish church to conform to English liturgical practice and church governance." [lxxx] The covenant was based on the King's Confession of 1581. [lxxxi] The National Covenant reinstated the foundations of the Reformed faith, but the covenant did not reject the king; rather, the covenant reaffirmed the need to stay loyal to the king. [lxxxii] It is a declaration of independence for the Scottish church, the faded copperplate script states the Scottish people's aspiration to political and ecclesiastical autonomy, free from the interference of kings and bishops.

Despite the people's protests and signing of the National Covenant in 1638, King Charles I was not swayed, and in retaliation for the riots, he ordered his army to put an end to the rebellion. The king's action prompted the beginning of the Bishops' Wars. The Bishop's War was one of the first of three major conflicts in the Wars of the Three Kingdoms. In the end, King Charles I would lose his head at the conclusion of the English Civil War and open the way for Oliver Cromwell to rise to power.

There are several handmade copies in existence, but this one is signed by the Marquis of Montrose, the Earl of Rother and Cassilis whose power was threatened by Charles's reforms. Many regard this document as the move away from ideas of divinely appointed rule towards participatory, modern democracy. The insistence on education for all, sowed the seeds of the Scottish Enlightenment. The National Covenant served as the foundation for the Declaration of Independence in America and drafting the US Constitution.

lxxxiii

*Bronze replica of stool Jenny Geddes*
*The Cutty Stool*
*Merilyn Smith Dedicated to Jenny Geddes 1637*
*By Scotswomen*

## Scottish Riots: From King Charles I to King Charles II

- Jenny Geddes Stool 1637
- Wars of the Covenant 1639-1651
- Wars of the 3 Kingdoms 1639-1651
- English Civil War 1642-1651
- Execution of King Charles I 1649
- Oliver Cromwell Occupation of Scotland 1653-1658
- Restoration of the Monarchy: King Charles II 1660

Although Jenny Geddes is believed to have been the trigger of the English Civil War, historians have found little evidence to confirm her role in the historic event in Scottish history. The lack of historical proof does not detract from the legacy. Robert Burns, a nationally recognized poet, was so moved by the story that he named his horse after Geddes in 1886. Today, as people come by and visit St. Giles Cathedral, a plaque located outside the Grand Cathedral reminds everyone of an amazing woman who used a three-legged stool to protest an injustice of her faith, which eventually ended with the king losing his head.

# Mercat Cross

lxxxiv

Free admission

High Street, Edinburgh, EH1 1RF, UK

Located in Parliament Square, along the Royal Mile, is an unusual octagonal-shaped structure with a platform and a rather tall spire placed in the middle. This uniquely shaped structure is known as the Mercat Cross (Market Cross). Dating back to William I (1165-1214)

71

the Mercat Cross served as an official marker of the king to authorize the town's trading status. The significance of the Mercat Cross was important to every town. If a town did not possess the Mercat Cross, it was forbidden to conduct business, make official decrees, host markets, auctions, or fairs. The tradition of having a Mercat Cross in town lasted well into the 17th century. During town market days, a heavy wooden arm was brought in to act as the official standard of measurement to weigh items sold in the market.

lxxxv

*Tron weighing scale.*

On top of the Mercat Cross is a platform used to make public announcements, general parliamentary election results, and the reading of wedding announcements, which were proclaimed at the location, and where official Crown business was discussed. From this platform, officials would announce the secession or death of the king. It would take three days for the town to receive the news. Although the Cross indicated the official decree of the king, the Cross also morphed into a place where the town would conduct business and punish criminals. Mild discipline for criminals could be something as simple as requiring a person to stand by the cross for a specified period with a paper stating the criminal actions committed by the person. More egregious criminal activities were also punished at the location. If an individual purchased an item from a market vendor and the customer believed they were tricked, the customer could legally challenge the vendor by weighing the item on the Tron Scale. If the vendor proved to be false in their dealings, the vendor would have his ear nailed to the wooden Mercat Cross. If the convicts did not want to wait until the sentence was fulfilled, they would choose to rip their ear away from the nail tacked to the cross and move on to another town. The term 'rip off' is derived from the dishonest vendors conducting business in the town markets. The ripped ear would distinguish an honest man from a dishonest one, serving as a warning to all potential customers. Additional harsher punishments, such as public hangings, the egging of criminals, and public burnings, were also held at the Cross.

lxxxvi

*Dismantled on March 13, 1756, and rebuilt in 1887.*

Since the 17th century, the current Mercat Cross has changed in both location and structure. By the 18th century, as Edinburgh was seeking to modernize, the Cross's octagonal structure became more of an obstruction for traffic in the city. The decision to tear down the old cross was approved in 1756, with different parts of the cross being stored at the Drum House in Gilmerton. The eight decorated plaques adorning the cross were bought by Sir Walter Scott, and he used them to decorate his Abbotsford House Garden walls.

74

lxxxvii

*1617-1715 location of the original Mercat Cross*

In 1866, the desire to rebuild the Mercat Cross began a growing movement to restore the lost history within the city, as many had come to regret the dismantling of the historic town centerpiece. Efforts to track down the old pieces were mostly successful. The Drum House had housed the 14-foot shaft, and Sir Walter Scott returned his plaques, but the unicorn that had once rested at the top of the shaft was nowhere to be found. Local artisans set out to reconstruct the missing unicorn from descriptions of the original design. The wooden base was rebuilt in 1885 out of stone to ensure its longevity. This part of the construction was financially sponsored by MP William Gladstone. For his donation, he was given the honor of writing an inscription in Latin, posted above the cross door.

"This ancient monument, the Cross of Edinburgh, which of old was set apart for public ceremonies, having been utterly destroyed by a misguided hand, and having been avenged as well as lamented, in song alike noble and manful, by the great man Walter Scott, has now, by favour of the Magistrates of the City, been restored by William Ewart Gladstone."

lxxxviii

Today, Mercat Cross has changed from its original wooden structure and taken on a different appearance. The location of the cross was also changed to make way for the modernization of the city. The new location of the cross is in Parliament Square. Public announcements are still made three days after the event from the platform on the Cross, and people gather to hear what is being proclaimed by the monarchy. On September 20, 2022, the passing of Queen Elizabeth II was announced from the Mercat Cross, and the accession of His Majesty the King was proclaimed.

# Old Tolbooth Prison

lxxxix

> High Street, Edinburgh,
> EH1 1RE, UK

The Old Tolbooth Prison was an imposing building located on the northwest corner of St. Giles' Cathedral. Although the prison was demolished in the 19th century, 400 years' worth of memories of the horrible conditions the prisoners endured; remain generations later. The original construction date of the Tolbooth is not known, but through archaeological discoveries, the prison has been dated back to as early as 1386. The Tolbooth prison was not initially designed to house criminals; instead, the building originally served the purpose

77

of a tax collection center and merchant market within the city of Edinburgh.

The Tolbooth bell informed the townspeople when the markets opened and called the counsel to meetings. The Tolbooth was used to conduct business and activities as well as house the local governing body. However, in 1560, the Tolbooth's role shifted when magistrates demanded the building be remodeled to accommodate better working conditions. Historical records indicate the transformation was a gradual process, beginning in the 1480s, with the first recorded mention of the building serving partially as a jail. By 1554, historical archives indicate the Tolbooth was expanded to serve as a new prison, coined the 'Thieves Hole'.[xc]

The expansion of the Tolbooth did not lead to improvements to the building. According to history, Mary Queen of Scots was astounded at the deplorable conditions and the nauseating smells emanating from the facilities where prisoners were held. She was so disgusted by the prison that she ordered the building to be torn down and rebuilt in 1561. After reconstruction, the prison continued to operate in its dual role as a government building and town prison, but by 1640 the Tolbooth was primarily used as the city's prison.

## Life as a prisoner in the Tolbooth Prison:

Throughout its long history the Tolbooth boasted a fearsome reputation for its hellish conditions and the brutal treatment of its prisoners. Judicial tortures and executions were commonplace at the Old Tolbooth. Attached to the west gable, was a protruding platform equipped with a gallow to allow Edinburgh's citizens view of all public hangings. Spikes were fixed into the stone jails to display the various body parts of those punished with the heaviest penalties. Included in this enviable roster was James Graham, 1st Marquis of Melrose, whose head was exhibited atop the Old Tolbooth for over ten years from 1650-1661. (Deacon Brodie was held here in 1788 before he was executed) In the latter years of the 17th century, prisoners would often be held at the Tolbooth before being banished to work on the American plantations.

## Interesting fact:

The Heart of Midlothian was placed at the entrance of the Old Tolbooth during its reconstruction, in 1561.

xci

The Old Tolbooth Prison served the City of Edinburgh until 1817, when the conditions of the building proved to be too run-down to save. During the same period, major changes within the city had also made the demolition of the building more desirable. In the 19th century, relic buildings were sacrificed in the name of modernity.  Furthermore, the Old Tolbooth was in the way during city expansion as residents moved into the area where the prison was occupied, known as 'the Luckenbooths'. With prisoners kept in the newer Calton Jail, the Tolbooth was considered obsolete and demolished.

Site of the Last Public Execution in Edinburgh
The site of the gallows is marked by the three brass plates set at the edge of the pavement in front of this notice. George Bryce, the Ratho Murderer, was executed here on 21st June 1864, the last public execution in Edinburgh.

xcii

Today, a reminder of the Tolbooth is marked with bronze bricks in the cobblestone street, outlining the parameters of the Old Tolbooth.  Furthermore, near Deacon Brodie's Pub are three bronze bricks marking the last prisoner, George Bryce execution spot on June 21, 1864.

# Heart of Midlothian

xciii

High Street, Edinburgh,
EH1 1RE, UK

Along the Royal Mile, near the west door of St. Gile Cathedral on High Street, a mosaic heart is embedded in the cobblestones. At first glance, this unique heart can easily be mistaken for a romantic story. The reality is that the Heart of Midlothian symbolizes a darker side of history. The heart is a marker for the Old Tolbooth (1386-1817), administration center and execution site in Edinburgh. The Heart of Midlothian is placed at the entrance of the old Tolbooth prison doors and serves as a reminder of the notorious history of one of the worst prisons in the UK. The reputation of the Old Tolbooth and what took place within the prison walls are legendary and evoke the most horrid images throughout the Empire.[xciv]

During the prison's reconstruction, in 1561, a heart was placed at the entry to serve as a memorial. It is not uncommon to witness a passerby lean over and spit on the mosaic heart (it is not illegal to do so). The spitting symbolizes spite against the loathsome and horrific deeds that still echo throughout the city's history. Over time, Scottish people began to view spitting on the heart as an act of good luck. Although now considered a form of good luck, a marriage proposal at the site is strongly discouraged and would be highly inappropriate. It would not be viewed as a romantic act.

Sir Walter Scott, the famous author from Edinburgh, was successful in obtaining the jail door of the Old Tolbooth for his Abbotsford home. Scott wrote stories about Scotland's past in his Waverly series. In one book, 'The Heart of Midlothian,' Scott writes about the historic event known as 'the Porteous Riots' that took place in 1736. This book uncovers the horrific things conducted behind Tolbooth's walls, rehashing the terrible suffering of prisoners who lived in the Empire's worst prisons.

# David Hume Statue

xcv

*(above) the arrow points to the famous 'Toe of Wisdom'*

379-381 High ST. Edinburgh, EH1 1PW, UK

David Hume, a philosopher, is known as one of the most influential men of the Scottish Enlightenment era. Hume was interested in the study of natural science, the government and its needs within society, empirical observation, and skepticism. According to his theories of economics, Hume is one of the most important philosophical writers of the English language. His studies were not limited to empiricism and skepticism, he also held firm beliefs on religion, superstition, and the reason of the human mind. One of his most notable beliefs rested in his theories of causation.[xcvi]

**David Hume - Empiricist:**
- Valued inductive reasoning.
- Scientific Method
- Mirroring John Locke's views on empiricism to an extreme.
- Simultaneously critical and favorable of Inductive Reasoning, although he also emphasized it.
- Problems of induction.
- Only valued views on reality if they were concerning human experience through senses.

[xcvii]

**Hume's' View on Causation:**

Hume saw causation as a relationship between two expressions or ideas in the mind. He argued that because causation is defined by experience, the cause-and-effect relationships cannot be proven due to the subjectivity of thoughts."

[xcviii]

David Hume's statue is imposing to see, but what catches people's eye is the large, shiny bronze toe looming above. This distinct polished bronze toe was intentionally designed by sculptor Alexander Stoddart. Hume's dangling foot over the edge of the base of the statues' platform inspired a superstitious tradition where people rub Hume's toe. They believed that wisdom or good luck would be bestowed upon them in exchange. Ironically, this form of ritual act would have been against Hume's belief that superstition was a corruption of true religion and was based on emotions gone wild.

# Well Heads

xcix

By 1681, water was brought into town through underground lead pipes from Castle Reservoir. A total of six cisterns, called Wellheads, supplied water for the locals in town. Only four of these cisterns remain today. Of the four, only two have the wellhead face on the cistern.[c]

In many ancient towns, water was vital to sustaining a community, and the town of Edinburgh was no different. Without the innovation of central plumbing, obtaining water was a laborious task for the citizens to retrieve water from Comiston Springs, castles reservoir, and transporting it back into town. Cisterns were an effective means to bring water into town.

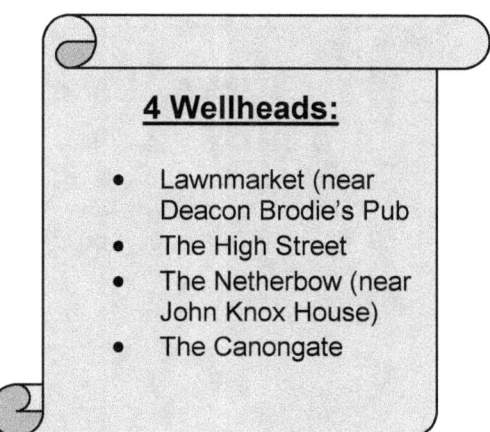

**4 Wellheads:**

- Lawnmarket (near Deacon Brodie's Pub
- The High Street
- The Netherbow (near John Knox House)
- The Canongate

The town of Edinburgh began experiencing population growth during the 1800s, and the six cisterns failed to produce enough water for the town. As a result, the water rations were implemented, limiting the hours of access to only three hours in a 24-hour period. Access was open from midnight to 3am. No one wanted to wake up in the middle of the night to retrieve water. Although an inconvenience, it provided an opportunity for citizens to earn extra income as water caddies for the wealthy. The growing population demands continued to pressure the water supplies pumped by the cisterns.[ci]

By the 19th century the wellheads fell into disuse as new water pumps were added to keep up with the demand of the growing population in the city. Today, the wellheads remain as a reminder of Edinburgh's past, but also serve as a popular tourist attraction.

### Interesting Fact:

The wellheads were the town gossip hotspots, much like today's modern water cooler is in an office building.

# Grassmarket

cii

Free admission

Grassmarket, Edinburgh,
EH1 2HY, UK

The Grassmarket is a popular place where markets display their goods. The history of Grassmarket dates to
1477, when it was the dominant marketplace in Edinburgh. The name "Grassmarket" was coined from the

grass and hay laid out in pens for the cattle and horses set for purchase.

The famed market was also witness to Edinburgh's darker history. The Grassmarket doubled as the site of public executions between 1661-1688 where 100 people lost their lives during the 'Killing Times'.[ciii] The Scottish Reformation brought about a clash between the Presbyterian Covenant movement and crown. The tragic history of the Killing Time prompted the people in Edinburgh to make a memorial of lives lost during this dark period in history. In 1937, the Gibbet was commissioned to represent the martyrs who died for their religious beliefs.

[civ]

*Gibbet Memorial*

Grassmarket made its mark in another significant part in history when the location was bombed in 1916 during WWI. A total of 11 people died in the bombing and in memory of the lives lost, a flagstone is placed on the pavement at the site of the bombing.

# King Charles II Statue

cv/cvi

Parliament Sq., Edinburgh,
EH1 1RE, UK

Along the Royal Mile, in Parliament Square, stands an unusual statue of a man in Roman garb astride a horse. The statue is of King Charles II of England, dressed in Roman military clothing, holding a baton designed to symbolize Imperial power. This easily begs the question, was King Charles II Roman?

King Charles was not actually Roman. The designer of his statue, Grinling Gibbons, was inspired by Marco Aurelius and the Romanesque style. In fact, there are two statues of King Charles II. The first statue

91

was completed in 1680 in Windsor, and the second was completed in 1685 in Edinburgh. Both statues were cast from the same mold, although the Windsor statue was cast in bronze, while Edinburg statue was cast in lead (believed to be the oldest lead statue in Britain).

The Edinburgh statue has not sustained well over the years. Due to the lead casting, the three thin legs of the horse were unable to support the massive weight of the statue. Multiple restoration efforts have been implemented to maintain the 325-year-old statue's structural integrity. In 1824, the statue was removed from Parliament Square. Ironically, this restoration work on the statue happened to be good luck, as it escaped the Great Fire in November 1824. The statue was stored away, and repairs were made to the broken leg in Calton Jail. A local surgical veterinarian, Dr. Dick, repaired the broken leg.[cvii]

**Henry Cockburn wrote in his Journal commenting on the restoration of the statue:**

May 12, 1835,

*I saw today for the first time the second Restoration of Charles II -I mean of his statue, which has been replaced in the Parliament Square after a sleep in the prison for eleven years. A very respectable piece of Art. The horse had cracked at the fetlocks, but his legs are now mended, and his other frailties solded, and his inside is sustained by a strong muscular system of oak, so he expected to defy the weather, and remain sound for another century. The little Parliament Close is now the most Continental-looking spot in Edinburgh.*

cviii

In 1877, the Scottish weather caused further damage to the statue. Cracks and splits began to appear, allowing rainwater to seep into the flanks of the horse. The wooden oak interior became compromised. This damage had quite an effect. The placement of the leaks caused the statue to appear to be urinating. In 2010, the statue was once again removed from the square for repair. Six months later, the horse returned to the square with a broader belly. The larger girth was an attempt to prevent rainwater from accumulating inside the horse. During the 2010 repair, a vacuum was placed inside the horses' stomach to remove the water leaking from the lead cracks. While mostly reliable, occasional leaking still occurs after heavy rain.[cix]

### Interesting Fact:

King Charles II was nicknamed 'Two-faced Monarch.' He promised to support the Presbyterian Scottish Movement in exchange for their support in placing him back on the throne. After being crowned king, he retracted his promise and instituted the Papacy in Scotland.

### Interesting fact:

Although Scotland declared Charles II King, England was under control of Oliver Cromwell, serving as de facto Republic. The Battle of Worcester (1651) forced Charles II to flee the country for 10 years. After the death of Cromwell, Charles II returned and ascended the throne to become the reigning monarch of England, Ireland, and Scotland by 1660.

[cx]

# James Braidwood

cxi

1-6 Parliament Square,
Edinburgh EH1 1RF, UK

A statue of James Braidwood stands in Parliament Square. The Englishman is situated with his fireman's hat in hand, admiring the city of Edinburgh. Braidwood's story is directly linked to the Great Fire of Edinburgh.

95

City fires have an uncanny ability to spread quickly from one building to the next, and within a short period of time, a whole block can be overtaken. Edinburgh, like many cities, was cramped with narrow roadways. Without modern understanding, many buildings were comparable to kindling. Since there were no interior sprinkler systems, or fire alarms, manpower to fight fires were essential for safety. The concept of a firefighting squad was first established by the Romans in 6 A.D with the Vigiles, the watchmen of the city. As such, the watchmen of Edinburgh were well established. After the Great Fire of London in the 1600s, the concept of fire insurance began to be the solution people were looking for. The first system put into place created multiple fire insurance companies. Families paid these companies to protect their homes in case of a fire. Each company had a special symbol placed on their insured homes. When fires broke out, firefighters contracted with the individual's fire insurance company were sent out. They extinguished the fire and doused the adjacent buildings as a precaution. This system worked for a time, but eventually the system's flaws couldn't be ignored.[cxii]

At the time, there were many fire insurance teams in the city, and they all competed against each other.   When a fire broke out in the city, the various fire insurance company men would arrive and check to see if the building was insured by their employer and if the neighboring facilities next to their insured home were safe.   After the insurance company determined their building was safe, the firefighters would stand by and do nothing to put the fire out near the insured structure. Other firemen would not help the competing fire teams.   Furthermore, different fire-insured companies would arrive at different times, and if a building's insurance company was late, then the building would remain burning.

Edinburgh was frustrated with the fire insurance system within the city and worked with James Braidwood to establish the fire brigade. Through considerable efforts and meticulous planning, the Braidwood system was based on scientific study and effective firefighting techniques. Two months after the birth of the Edinburgh Fire Brigade, the Great Fire of Edinburgh erupted.

On November 15, 1824, in the old Assembly Close building, a fire started on the 2nd floor of James Kirkwood Engravers shop. The Fire Brigade quickly arrived at the location but soon realized that they had an insufficient water supply. After an hour of searching for a water source, the fire had consumed six floors of the building and was still spreading rapidly. By the next day, the fire's destructive path had reached Tron Kirk. Twenty-four hours after the fire began, the fire had encompassed Parliament Square and fears of the fire jumping across the Royal Mile to overtake St. Giles Cathedral became a growing concern. By this time, all hands-on decks were made to save the church.

By November 21, 1824, the Fire Brigade's efforts began to contain the fire. Inquiries were immediately raised as to why the newly formed Fire Brigade failed to prevent the fire from spreading. After an investigation, the truth of the failure was revealed. The old laws, established during the fire-insurance period limited the brigade's ability to act as they should have. The Brigade had no cohesive plan to act without a single leader taking charge. The insured homeowners, insured firefighters, and city officials believed they had the authority to order the Brigade around. Amid the confusion, the fire continued to rage, while the men ran frantically around trying to follow all the orders they were given. After the investigation, the city of Edinburgh placed James Braidwood in charge of the Fire Brigade. Officials removed the rules that had hindered the men from performing their job effectively. Through vision and intentional leadership, Braidwood established a system where all firefighters were trained in the procedures of firefighting, worked together as a unit, and utilized the latest scientific technology to fight fires throughout the world.[cxiii] The success of his firefighters quickly spread to London. On January 1, 1833, Braidwood was asked to establish his firefighting system in the city of London. Within a short period of time, Braidwood's Fire Brigade format soon spread throughout the world.

On June 22, 1861, a fire broke out on the dockside warehouse on Tooley Street along the south side of the Thames in England. As Braidwood ran into the building to lead his men in the fight, the building collapsed on him. He died at age 61. His funeral, a week later, had one of the largest gatherings of people paying their respects to a man who had accomplished so much for the country and the world through his scientific approach in firefighting. Today, his legacy is memorialized in a statue of a man who keeps vigilant watch over the city of Edinburgh, waiting for his call to save lives.

# Adam Smith

cxiv

192 Royal Mile, Edinburgh, EH1 1RF, UK

Located in the heart of Edinburgh's Royal Mile stands the 10-foot statue of Adam Smith, unveiled on July 4, 2008. Smith is known as the Great Scottish Economist and Philosopher and is the author of the famed book *The Wealth of Nations*. Created by Alexander Stoddart, the imposing statue depicts Smith in his later years looking toward Canongate, where he is buried.

Adam Smith is credited with inventing modern economics by challenging 18th-century economic laissez-faire liberalism. [cxv] This form of economic theory is based upon the looser market strategy of 'let it be'. Adam Smith introduced new theories on how a fair economy should operate based upon the notion that "self-interested people naturally end up working toward an outcome that benefits everyone." [cxvi] His theories of natural liberty and the 'invisible hand' changed the previous economic theory into the current economic theory used today. Smith introduced the idea of capitalism through the ideas of specialization and division of labor to achieve wealth (macroeconomics theory). His beliefs and contributions to the field of economics earned him the title 'Father of Economics.'

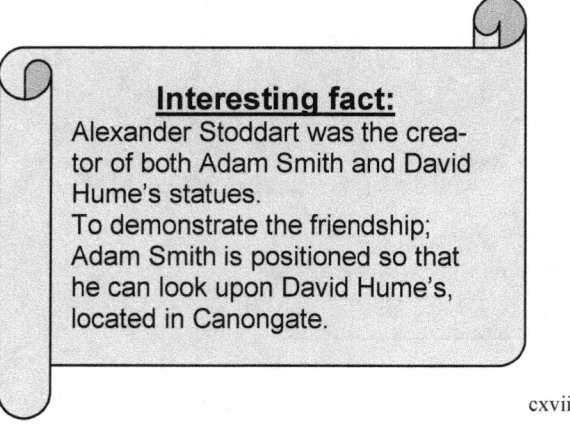

**Interesting fact:**
Alexander Stoddart was the creator of both Adam Smith and David Hume's statues.
To demonstrate the friendship; Adam Smith is positioned so that he can look upon David Hume's, located in Canongate.

cxvii

Adam Smith's statue features a beehive above a stalk of corn by his side. Both images symbolize industry in an agrarian society. Located behind Smith is a simple farming plow. This symbolizes a decline in agrarian economics considering the Industrial Revolution sweeping across the nation at the time.

# Statue Cones

cxviii

*Adam Smith statue coned.*

Walking through Edinburgh, an unusual object might make an appearance. A traffic cone rests on top of a statue's head. It would be easy to assume that this indicates that the statue is marked for repair, but this is not the case.

Beginning in the 1980s, throughout Glasgow and Edinburgh, cones atop local statues have become a common sight. There are two possible reasons why the cones appeared. The first theory is that people, getting drunk and wanting to have fun in the wee hours of the night, found construction traffic cones that marked off sections on the road and decided to place the cones on the statues' heads. The second theory suggests the cone-ing of statues began with pranksters having a bit of fun.

The city officials do not approve of the use of traffic cones to decorate the city's famous statues. One of the main reasons is that the cones decrease tourist viewing of the statues. Each year, the cost of removing the cones is estimated to be about $10,000. While it is easy to place the cones on the heads of statues, the removal requires a series of safety precautions to protect the workers.

The cone wars between the residents and city officials have been going on for the past 40 years and do not show any signs of ending. The cone-ing of statues has become a local cultural phenomenon. With a unique twist, the cones have become a custom where residents have taken ordinary traffic cones and decorated them before secretly placing the unique cones on the heads of statues. Some residents have gone as far as using the cones to advertise political beliefs and points of view.

Either way, the battle between the locals and city officials continues, and the city is losing the battle of the cones. When a cone is placed on the statues, the city acts quickly to remove them from view. Like many traditions in Edinburgh, the cone-ing of statues has evolved into a newer tradition. Tourists have come to visit Edinburgh and Glasgow with the hope of witnessing the cone-ing of statues. If you are lucky, you may be able to spot the cone that adorns the heads of statues as you walk through the city of Edinburgh. You might even be lucky enough to see a tri-cone statue. [cxix]

# Mary King's Close

cxx

> $$$ admission

> High St., 2 Warriston's Cl,
> Edinburgh, EH1 1PG, UK

During the 17th century, life in Edinburgh was not ideal. Overpopulation soared, and people crammed together in skyscraper homes. As mentioned earlier, the sanitary conditions in the city were in a state of crisis, with no solution to the growing sewer and waste removal problems. Without modern plumbing, people would throw their waste onto the streets below. The grooves in the cobblestone pavement drained into Nor Loch and polluted the local lake on the northern side of Edinburgh Castle. The conditions set the stage for one of the worst plagues in world history. Rats ran wild throughout the city, rapidly multiplying off the waste produced. Lacking modern medical knowledge; there was little understanding of the consequences facing the people. When the Black Plaque began devastating England, the Scottish people falsely believed they would be spared. They were bold enough to mock the English, proclaiming "the foul death of the English." [cxxi] Soon, the Scotts would come to regret their arrogance and suffer the catastrophe of the Black Plague in their country.

The Old Town in Edinburgh was hit particularly rougher than the New Town, but neither section was truly spared. Old Town quickly witnessed the ravaging effects of the plague due to the compact living conditions that many families were forced to endure. The residence of Mary King's Close was hit particularly hard due to the underground location, dark and damp living conditions, poor sanitation, and the abundance of rat colonies.

Ideas on how to combat the black plaque were suggested. One story circulating throughout history was the City Council's solution to quarantine the residence of Mary King's Close, thus sealing the fate of the 600 people who lived in the Close in 1644. [cxxii] This story is proven to be a myth. The town council had gone to great lengths to care for the people within the city and sought efforts to demonstrate compassion for the victims. Healthy members were relocated to Burgh Muir, and families suffering from the effects of the plague would post a white flag in the windows of homes to warn workers of their conditions. Workers would come by and bring food and coal, placing the needed goods outside the door so the residents could retrieve the supplies to sustain them.

cxxiii

The Plague Doctor, Dr. George Rae, adorned himself in leather covering his entire body, and upon his head he wore a beak-shaped mask. The mask was to serve as protection against the plague. De l'Orme described the plague doctor's outfit worn to aid in protecting him from contracting the plague during his care of infected patients infected:

"The nose [is] half a foot long, shaped like a beak, filled with perfume... Under the coat, we wear boots made in Moroccan leather (goat leather) ...and a short-sleeved blouse in smooth skin ...The hat and gloves are also made of the same skin...with spectacles over the eyes."

cxxiv

While the outfit looks bizarre by today's standards, the crude garb did work. The leather gown prevented the fleas from biting Dr. Rae, and the beak mask may have diffused the spread of the virus. Rae's attempt to combat the virus was basic at best. He would use a fire poker and cauterize the open wound caused by the pus-filled cyst to prevent infection and spread of the virus. This crude procedure did succeed in saving lives. George Rae survived the Black Plague and saved many people in Edinburg with his primitive medical treatment.

The Close remained as a place of residence until 1902, when the last person decided to move elsewhere. The city sealed off the Close and remained empty throughout the 20th century. During WWII, the Close was reopened and used as a bomb shelter, but it was forgotten until a workman mistakenly knocked a wall down in 2003. The hidden close was once again brought back from history, and the stories of the people who resided in the underground location were brought back to life. Today, people can visit Mary King's Close through local tour guides. [cxxv]

# The Vault

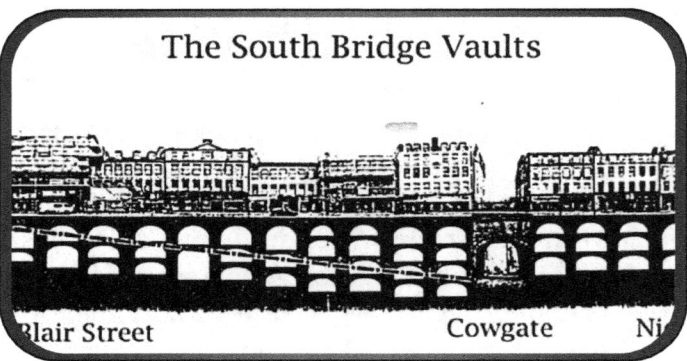

The South Bridge Vaults

Blair Street          Cowgate          N|

cxxvi

> $$$ admission

> Mercat Tours 28 Blair Street,
> Edinburgh, EH1 1QR, UK

Constructed on a dormant volcano plug, Edinburgh's design over the years has transformed the landscape of the city. Edinburgh is a city that is mounted on seven hills. Castle Hills and Carlton Hill are two of the seven hills that remain visible today, but as the city changed during the 18th century, a series of five bridges were added to bypass the valleys between the hills.

Of the five bridges running through Edinburgh, two are more commonly known: the South Bridge and the North Bridge. The South Bridge connects Old Town's High Street to the nearby university located in the southern section of the city.

In 1785, the expansion of the Old Town of Edinburgh into the New Town involved connecting the hills surrounding the city. A series of 19 stone arches were constructed, stretching a 1,000-feet-long gap between two hills, and filling the valley below. This was a feat of engineering for its time, as great efforts were made to overcome obstacles in the terrain. The stone arches ranged in height to level out the bridges connecting the hills, with the lowest arch standing 31 feet above the ground. To secure the structural integrity, engineers anchored the bridge arches 22 feet below the bedrock underground. [cxxvii] After the completion of the South Bridge in 1788, businessmen began moving their shops to the bridge. In addition to the store, rental property was also added to maximize the space along the bridge. All the buildings were built on top of the 19 arches. City planners thought to utilize the spaces below the bridge within the 19 arches. The arch enclosures became vaulted chambers beneath the bridge, creating the storage space the businesses needed. As such, the businesses were also able to use the space below to establish underground professions such as taverns, cobblers, cutlers, smelters, victualers, and milliners.[cxxviii] No space was wasted, and it was a great idea in theory. However, Scotland's rain did not mix well with the arches at ground level. The natural elements seeped into the porous stone structure, causing frequent leaks and constant moisture. With ruined merchandise, the shopkeepers decided to abandon the vaults. The businesses above continued to operate, and life went on as normal. Eventually, people forgot about the vaults below.

Without any active businesses in the area, the homeless moved in and began to operate underground. The vaults also became a refuge for many of the Scottish clans hiding out after the Battle of Culloden. Over time, the sanitary conditions and criminal activity worsened. This spurred the city to clear out and fill in the vaults, preventing further illegal activities. A chance discovery in 1985 reinstated the vaults in history when a college student accidentally knocked out the back of his kitchen cabinet and was shocked to discover a hidden world behind his wall.

Today, the only visible remains of the South Bridge arches are located at Cowgate. Visitors and locals can walk through the vaults and see how people once lived in an underground city. Mercat Tours conducts these tours. They do an outstanding job at recounting and reviving the vaults' history. Since tour slots fill quickly, advanced reservations are strongly encouraged. During Halloween, Mercat Tours offers a special ghost tour of the underground vaults.

# Alexander & Bucephalus Statue

[cxxix] *Alexander, the Great, turning Bucephalus toward the Sun.*

Edinburgh, EH1 1BN, UK

Alexander (The Great) Bucephalus statue is a remarkable statue to admire. The statue captures a popular legend of a 12-year-old Alexander the Great winning a bet with his father, Philip II of Macedon. The story begins with a Thessalian horse dealer, [cxxx] petitioning Alexander's father to purchase the Thessalian stallion for a substantial fee. As Philip II observed the horse's unstable, wild behavior, he decided to decline. Young Alexander, determined to have that horse, struck a deal

111

with his father. Alexander told his father that he would tame the wild horse, and if he failed, he would pay the price for the horse. An agreement was made, and young Alexander approached the wild horse, speaking softly to the agitated stallion. Alexander realized the horse wasn't as wild as people thought. He was frightened by his shadow. Alexander coaxed the horse to face the sun so the shadow would no longer be seen.

The stallion calmed, and shortly after their encounter, Alexander tamed the wild horse and won the bet. Alexander named the horse Bucephalus (Greek for Ox-head said to be a solid black horse with a large star on his forehead). The bond between rider and horse lasted for two decades. Bucephalus and Alexander worked together, winning battles and conquering lands, to build the' Great Empire' from 355 to 326 B.C. In the last battle Alexander fought, Bucephalus was fatally wounded and died. Alexander founded the city of Bucephala (believed to be modern-day Jhelum, Pakistan) in honor of his favorite horse. [cxxxi]

Alexander's Bucephalus statue symbolizes the triumph of intelligence over brute force. The bronze statue was created by John Steell in 1832. Steell, a perfectionist, spent years creating the sculpture and eventually ran out of funds to complete his work. Unable to fund the bronze casting, the statue sat for 50 years until 1883. Bucephalus was unveiled in 1884 and placed toward the sun so that the statue would never see its shadow.

*cxxxii*

*On the right the arrow points to Bucephalus pig-shaped ears.*

John Steell was paid 100 guineas with the addition of funds gathered from donations. It is believed the full payment was not paid for 50 years. When the statue was unveiled in 1884 in St. Andrew's Square, the horse had a noticeable flaw in its appearance. Bucephalus, the war horse, had ears shaped like pigs' ears. The obvious mistake is believed to have been intentional. Many theorize that John Steell decided to give the stallion pigs ears right before the sculpture was cast in bronze out of spite for not getting paid in full. While no one knows for certain, this is the story people have believed over the years. In 1916, Bucephalus was relocated to the City Chambers.

# The Tron Kirk

cxxxiii /cxxxiv

*Public weighing scale next to the Tron Kirk*

Free admission

122 High Street, Edinburgh, EH1 1SG, UK

Often overshadowed by the beauty of St. Giles Cathedral, but not any less significant, is the infamous Tron Kirk located on the Royal Mile. Tron Kirk dates back nearly 400 years, when King Charles I commissioned its construction in 1637. The Kirk opened for worship in 1641, although construction wasn't complete until 1647.[cxxxv] John Mylne, inspired by contemporary Dutch design, fashioned the building in the shape of the

114

letter 'T'. The church was dedicated to Christ and nicknamed 'Christ's Kirk at the Tron', although eventually the name was simplified to 'The Tron'. The simplified name is derived from the name of the Salt-Tron, a public weighing beam (see the drawing above the Tron Kirk image) that was located outside the building. The Tron was the central gathering point where the public met to exchange goods, weigh items, and punish criminals.

In 1785, John Baxter redesigned the church. He altered the structure from a 'T' shape to a rectangle to make way for the building of South Bridge and Hunter Street. In order to construct the North and South Bridges, sections of the church were demolished to connect Old Town Edinburgh and New Town Edinburgh.

In 1824, a fire burned down the original wooden spire on the Tron. The spire, added in 1671, by Thomas Sandilands, was replaced with an octagonal stone spire commissioned by Richard and Robert Dickson. In 1888, Robert Rowand Anderson focused his restoration efforts on the Tron interior, constructing a new pulpit and gallery. Anderson's design likely includes the beautiful stained-glass windows within the kirk.

The Tron acted as a kirk until 1952, when the members of the kirk relocated to another church building. The city of Edinburgh's Council purchased the kirk from the Church of Scotland. For 22 years, the building remained unused by the city. The building, originally the center of town, began to show its wear after surviving major fires, riots, two World Wars, and harsh Scottish weather. Efforts to restore the old church began in 1974 and lasted for two years. Initially, restoration was planned to repair the steeple, but upon further investigation, archaeologists discovered an older part of Scottish history. They found Marlin's Wynd under the foundations of the church. The archaeologists estimate Marlin's Wynd to be the oldest cobblestone path in Scottish history.

The Tron's restoration was not completed, and the building remained empty. In 2003, Tron was added to the risk registry. Efforts to use the building were short-lived. Attempts to make the Tron a bookshop, a festival market, and a local tourist information building all failed.

The Edinburgh World Heritage Trust leased the Tron from December 2018 to 2020 to revitalize the historic structure. The Tron no longer serves as a place of worship. Instead, it has been transformed into an artist marketplace, highlighting local artisans and vendors with an array of jewelry, woodwork, glass designs, and original artwork.

Today, the city of Edinburgh Council has listed Tron Kirk as a Scottish Historic Building along the Edinburgh Royal Mile (SHBT). SHBT has become the new caretaker of the old Kirk. With a new five-year lease and partnership with the city council, SHBT's restoration efforts have allowed the old kirk to be cherished once again by locals and tourists alike. After the five-year lease ends, SHBT hopes to extend their lease to 125 years and continue their efforts to maintain the kirk for the 21st century. [cxxxvi]

# Lady Stair's Close & Writer's Museum

cxxxvii

*Plaques, throughout the courtyard display famous Scottish writers and quotes.*

Free admission

Lady Stair's Close,
Lawnmarket Royal Mile,
Edinburgh. EH1 2PA. UK

Just off Lawnmarket, one can find Lady Stair's Close. The narrow close transports visitors into Edinburgh's past with fairytale-like buildings located in an open courtyard by the popular Writer's Museum. This hidden gem is often overlooked by visitors, who are unaware of the picturesque world beyond the entrance.

117

Once inside, they will discover the 17th-century townhouse of Lady Stair's. Originally built in 1622 by Sir William Gray of Pittendrum, the townhouse was not always known as Lady Stair's. Instead, the building used to be referred to as Lady Gray's House, dating back to the original owners' widow.

The original owner of the townhouse was a wealthy merchant who was incredibly successful in his career. During the early 17th century, it was not uncommon for the wealthier class citizens to have their homes hidden from the view of the public. This would allow the family to remain relatively undisturbed by the hustle and bustle of the city while remaining near their place of business. This is why Lady Stair's Close is removed from the beaten path of the Royal Mile. For Sir William Gray of Pittendrum, his seclusion from the city would not keep him from experiencing the turbulence of the Scottish Civil War in 1640. Sir Gray, like many others caught up in the storm of war, would find himself sent to prison in Edinburgh Castle due to his ties with the Royalist side in the war. To make matters worse, in 1645, his daughter had fallen victim to the plague that had been sweeping throughout the region. Brokenhearted at the loss of his daughter and financially ruined, Sir Gray passed away in 1648. He left behind his wife, who lived many years after her husband's passing. The townhouse became known as Lady Gray Close in honor of her.

By 1719, the townhouse was purchased by John Dalrymple, the 1st Earl of Stairs, and the townhouse became known as Lady Stair's Townhouse. With the expansion of the city, many wealthier merchants moved to New Town and left their homes abandoned. By 1890, Lady Stair's Townhouse had become another victim of neglect. Lord Rosebery took a chance and purchased the old townhouse in 1893. The home had some sentimental value for him, as he was the direct descendant of Sir William Gray. Rosebery undertook a major demolition to save his ancestral home, with the guidance of restorationist George Shaw Aitken. Major changes were made to alter the building's original design. To save the home, portions of the building had to be torn down, leaving behind a section of the building. cxxxviii

With sections of the building removed, the need to add architectural flair became the focal point of the restoration. Elegant turrets were added to the building, and the 17th-century design highlighted the era of the time. Though changes had to be made, Rosebery made a great effort to maintain much of the original design. Visiting the townhouse, one can still admire the 400-year history of the building. As fashionable of its time, the entrance is adorned with a stone lintel with the date of 1622 and the initials of the original owner, Sir William Gray, and his wife, Geida Smith, inscribed.

cxxxix

By 1907, the house was given to the city of Edinburgh for the sole purpose of using the home as a museum, but this was short-lived, as once again the home was returned to the family in 1937. The townhouse seemed to be a house set aside for widows, and once again another widow and her two children became owners of the home.

Today the building is back in the hands of the city and has become a Writer's Museum celebrating the famous writers and poets of Scotland: Sir Walter Scott, Robert Louis Stevenson, Robert Fergusson, John Muir, John Barbor, and Robert Burns, to name a few. Within the courtyard, along the pathway, are about 38 concrete slabs embedded in the ground of famous people's quotes surrounding the museum. Lady Stair's Close is a popular tourist site, if one knows where to look, off the beaten path of Lawnmarket. Like all museums in Scotland, the Writer's Museum is free to all visitors. Take time to admire the building and the grounds below and discover famous Scottish people along the way.

This is my own, my native land
Sir Walter Scott (1771 - 1832)

there are no stars so lovely
as Edinburgh street-lamps
Robert Louis Stevenson
(1850 - 1894)

Auld Reikie
wale o ilka town
ROBERT FERGUSSON (1750-1774)

I care to live only to entice people
to look at Nature's loveliness.
John Muir 1838 - 1914

Fredome
is a noble thing
John Barbour
(c.1320-1395)

cxl

# Gladstone's Land

cxli

$$$ admission

477B Lawnmarket, Edinburgh, EH1 2NT, UK

Located east of Edinburgh Castle and west of St. Giles Cathedral is a building called Gladstone's Land. Gladstone's Land dates to 1550, much like the rest of the area, but what makes this specific building unique is the intentional efforts made to preserve its historical integrity. The interior designs have been carefully conserved and capture the distinctive artistry of the time.

In this building, visitors can experience the living conditions and transitions of multiple time periods in a single location. There are no doubt Edinburgh hosts old and medieval buildings depicting the history of the 1,000 years in Edinburgh, but Gladstone's Land presents the opportunity for visitors today to experience the living conditions of three distinct time periods.

The history of Gladstone's Land takes place in the 16th century when a wealthy merchant by the name of Thomas Gladstone purchased the building in 1617. The iconic golden hawk (gled) was placed above the exterior of the door, and additional floors above the family's residence were used to house tenements. Thomas Gladstone's renovation efforts expanded the footprint of the building by doubling the available space in front of the structure and extending the perimeter by 7 meters toward Lawnmarket. During the remodeling, Thomas Gladstone installed large stone arcades on the foundation of the floor to enable proper support for the oversized chambers located on the upper floors, and he encased a couple of business shops below.

Thomas and his wife left a lasting memorial to their ownership of the building. Up on the gables lie two carved initials, TG (Thomas Gledstone) and BC (Bessie Cunnungham). By the 18th century, Edinburgh had expanded its borders from the Old Town to the New Town. When New Town was built, many of the wealthier merchants relocated to the newer section of Edinburgh, leaving their homes behind. As the wealthy people moved out of the historic buildings, the lower-income residents quickly filled the abandoned homes. Lower-income residents were unable to maintain the cost of updating the buildings, and Gladstone's Land, like many buildings of the day, fell into disrepair. Efforts to bring the city into the 18th century promoted the notion of tearing down old relics of the past to make room for modernization. The area of Lawnmarket became one of the principal areas in which demolition was conducted, but Gladstone's Land managed to avoid destruction in 1895. By 1934, the building had become so hazardous that the city deemed it too dangerous to maintain. Gladstone was scheduled for demolition, but the National Trust of Scotland came to the rescue and purchased the property from the city.

During the reconstruction of the first two floors, the National Trust of Scotland discovered a goldmine of history. The rebuilding became a scavenger hunt to uncover the hidden secrets preserved in the building. After years of being neglected, the detailed, hand-painted ceilings were preserved. Restorationists uncovered Gladstone's intentional efforts to create a functioning home, business, and rental facility. On the ground floor, preservationists discovered an arcade [cxlii] used to protect the shop floors from wearing down. Located on the left side of the building, a spiral staircase opening access to the 2nd -4th floors of the building were uncovered. Under the stairs, preservationists came across the remains of a pig pen where pigs could forage food on the streets of Edinburgh. [cxliii]

The completed restoration provides interesting insight into the world of three people in the era of the world they lived in. [cxliv]

## Margaret Noble & John Riddock - 17th century (1st Floor)

Depicts life during the 17th century of the Thomas Gladstone home with renters John Riddock and Margaret Noble who were wealthy spice Traders.

On the 1st floor, visitors can explore the 1620 Scottish Renaissance period with a kitchen and storage room and peek into the life of a family of 7 with 5 children and 2 servants.

## Elizabeth Pillan & William Dawson- 18th century (2nd Floor)

Depicts The family business in tapestries displaying the historic fabrics, haberdashery, and fashion accessories of the elites in society during the 18th century.

The Georgian themes floor display the Gilded period in Scottish history.

## Mary Wilson -20th century (3rd Floor)

Depicts life in the 20rth century through the venue of Mary Wilson.

Reconstruction of the boarding house she ran. Although the home had already begun to deteriorate, Ms. Wilson managed to make the home a decent place to live for the 2 or 3 respectable men who rented the quarters.

A time-travel capsule of history, Gladstone's Land is a must-see for visitors with a fondness for history in the city.

cxlv

On the exterior of the building, above the door frame, is a golden hawk looming above as people pass underneath. The golden hawk represents Thomas's family name, Gled, which means hawk. Another notable feature of the exterior is that the top portion of the building's windows are covered with wooden panels. This discovery tells a simple story of value over economics. When Thomas Gledstone was remodeling his building, he viewed the purchase of glass as an excess cost. To provide his home with glass windows and save on the overall cost, he opted to only use glass panels for the upper levels and wooden panels for the base level.

# Paisley Close

cxlvi

97 High Street, Edinburgh,
EH1 1SG, UK

Along the Royal Mile, near John Knox's house, is a
stone statue of a young boy forever memorialized
above Paisley Close. This close is unique out of the 80
closes for its impact on the history of Edinburgh. The
story of Paisley Close began with a baker in the building. The lower portion of the building was the bakery,
and the higher levels housed tenements (renters). The
baker wanted to expand his oven and decided to 'do it

127

yourself, DIY' without any building or construction experience. It was a DIY gone wrong. Without knowing it, the baker knocked down a structural support wall on November 24, 1861. The building collapsed. A total of 77 people were housed in the building, and 35 were pronounced dead. The city people rallied to aid the people stuck in the sunken building and tried to dig them out. By the evening, townspeople began giving up hope of finding any more survivors. They started to turn away when suddenly a small voice could barely be heard, pleading for the people not to give up. Eventually, the crowd could make out a child's voice shouting, "Heave away, lads, heave away! I'm not dead yet!" With renewed energy the city folks started searching for the child behind the voice. They successfully pulled out 12-year-old Joseph McIver from the rumble.

With the loss of 35 people, the Edinburgh City Chambers enacted the City Improvement Act ordering all unsafe buildings to be torn down. The law substantially changed the blueprint of the Royal Mile and reduced the number of dangerous closes along the main road of the city. Of 245 closes, wynds, and courts, only 80 remain, although all are not accessible by the public. As a tribute to Joseph McIver, the city contracted the boy's face as a part of the memorial to the lives lost in November 1861.[cxlvii]

# John Knox House

cxlviii

$$$ admission

High Street, Edinburgh,
EH1 1SR, UK

The Royal Mile is a spectacular walk through the history of Scotland and has housed many amazing people who shaped the world they lived in. One such individual was a man by the name of John Knox. He is known as the father of the Scottish Reformation Movement. His house, constructed in 1470, still stands along the Royal Mile. John Knox's house commemorates the history and impact he had in Edinburgh.

cxlix

The history of the house begins with a tale of two men with opposing religious beliefs. The first part of the story begins with a man named Mossman and his wife, Mariotta Arries. Their home was included as part of Mariotta's dowry. Above the door, their initials are carved over the Mossman's coat of arms. Inscribed on the lintel is the motto (LYFE: GOD ABVFE ALTAND • YI-NYCHTEOVROOS), which can be translated as "Love God Above Your Neighbor As Yourself".[cl]

The story of James Mossman is one that reflects the religious turbulence between Scotland and England. Mossman was a jeweler and a goldsmith by trade, but he also held a higher role in the town as Keeper of the Royal Mint. His allegiance was pledged to Mary, Queen of Scots. As such, he was a devout Catholic. Mossman had a respectable life and held favor with the crown. This changed rather abruptly when Queen Mary was forced to abdicate the throne on July 24, 1567. Within a short period of time, his position in the community took a drastic turn and altered his life forever.

130

With Queen Mary removed from power, Mossman decided to join the rebellion against the new, protestant government. By the end of the long siege, the Protestant fighters had won and forced Queen Mary's loyal supporters to surrender the castle. On their surrender, her followers were condemned as traitors and forced to forfeit all their property. Mossman lost his beloved home because of his loyalty to the Queen. In an ironic twist of fate, John Knox, a man who played a major role in Queen Mary's removal, moved into Mossman's home.

John Knox's life began in Haddington, close to Edinburgh. He was even trained as a priest. However, he eventually came to believe the Catholic Church needed reform. His views did not go over well with the Catholic leaders. This opposition led him away from Catholicism to a more Protestant outlook. Deeply convicted, Knox's passion ignited the Protestant Reformation. Through public debates, his zeal touched the Scottish people. With a fiery passion, he sought to reform the church and lead the movement to remove the queen from power. Within the walls of St. Giles Cathedral, Knox could be heard preaching the Word of God and bringing the corruption of the Catholic Church to light.

The location of Mossman's home served as an ideal location for the elderly Knox. Although no known record has been discovered of his passing, historians believe Knox only resided in the house for the last three months of his life in 1572. The story of the two men and one house seemed to disappear from history as Old Town Edinburgh slowly lost its significance during the 17th and 18th centuries. In 1850, the Church

131

of Scotland came to the rescue. As an attempt to save the Old Town's history, the dilapidated building became a museum dedicated to Knox's role in the Scottish Reformation. Although historians were uncertain if Knox had resided in the home.

## Interesting Fact:

Although historians were uncertain if Knox had resided in the home; the excavation of his home, in 1840, discovered 2-time capsules were discovered in the gable walls which confirmed his residence in the home.

cli/clii

The story of John Knox does not end with his home being preserved. While Knox's home was rescued, his burial site remained a mystery for centuries.

Knox's grave was always believed to have resided near St. Giles Cathedral, but the church had also undergone changes. Over the years, many theories about the exact location of Knox's burial grounds have been debated. According to an old expansion plan on the church property, it is likely that the location of Knox's grave is in the parking lot of St. Giles. To accommodate needed parking, the old cemetery was cemented to expand parking. No one knows if it was intentional to pave over his grave, but either way, Number 23 is the accepted grave site of Knox and serves as an active parking space in the parking lot. Initially, a plaque marked the gravesite, but when a car parked in the spot, no one could see the plaque. As a result, a second plaque was added outside the parking space for people to easily see Knox's grave site.[cliii]

### Interesting Fact: St. Giles dogs

John Knox's friend John Craig told Knox about his adventure traveling on his way home. Along the journey, Craig was struck with a severe illness. Near death, Craig claimed that a dog saved his life. (Vague in detail of how it transpired) the story promoted Knox to allow dogs to roam freely at St, Giles Church and the tradition is still practiced today.

[cliv]

# Tweeddale Court

clv

14 High Street, Edinburgh,
EH1 1TE, UK

Tweeddale Court is one of the closes along the Royal
Mile dating back to 1576. The court's namesake was
the Marquess of Tweeddale, who served as senior advisor. The building is believed to have served as a
Georgian-era sedan-chair house garage. Sedan chairs
were brought to London in 1634 by Sir Saunders Dun-
combe. The sedan chairs provided a cheaper, safer, and
healthier form of travel for passengers through the
muddy, filth-ridden streets. The sedan consisted of a
seat box with two long poles posed at the base. Two
men, one posted in the front and the other in the back,
called, 'chairmen', would carry the passenger throughout town to the desired location. The Sedan Chair was
convertible with an easy-to-remove top to allow for additional head space for the extravagant dressing styles
of the wealthier class.

clvi

The chairmen were like modern-day taxi drivers and were required to obtain a license to travel. Like a taxi driver, the chairmen were available for hire at any time, including after midnight, which of course substantially increased the price. The extra fee was to pay the link boys who ran ahead of the chairman at night, lighting the way for safe travel. Interestingly, the sedan chairs had the right of way on the pavement. Phrases such as 'Have a care!' or 'By your leave, sir!' were common terms used to make way as the sedan traveled along townspeople's walkways. Although the chairman had the right of way, occasional accidents happened as the men traveled through the busy streets. Thus, traveling in the sedan chairs was convenient but not entirely safe. Furthermore, being carried with a top-heavy box on two poles often causes the riders to bounce around and tip over. By the 19th century, improvements in the city's sanitation conditions had improved, and the demand for sedan chairs had declined. The Tweeddale building is believed to be a lasting structure where the sedan chairs were housed in Edinburgh.

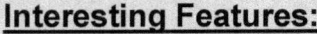

### Interesting Features:

Two features to look for when walking through Tweeddale Court:

- The King's Wall marker that denotes the original city boundaries.
- The remnants of the first gas-powered future in Scotland - located at the entrance of the court.

# World's End

clvii

Free admission

12 High Street, Edinburgh,
EH1 1SG, UK

Further down the Royal Mile lies a royal blue close entitled 'World's End Close'. The close does not refer to
the Pirates of the Caribbean movie, but instead a period
in Edinburgh's past when the city had been walled in.
During the Battle of Flodden in 1513, Scottish King
James IV perished, city officials became deeply concerned that additional English attacks would continue
after the loss of the battle. The solution was to erect a
24-foot wall, surrounding 140 acres, around the city to
protect the citizens, about 10,000 residents. The wall

137

was finished in 1560 with six ports to guard against un-desirable guests, like smugglers, from entering the city gates. Although the English troops never launched an-other attack, other outside enemies sought to besiege the castle throughout the 16th century. One of the can-nons that remains today, Mons Meg, is credited with destroying a building outside the wall used by snipers when the castle was attacked.[clviii] Most residents never ventured out of the gates. Even if they did leave, to re-enter the city, they were charged a fee. To those living behind the wall, it must've felt like the end of the world. Very few residents could afford the re-entry fee, so they never left the gates of the town.

# Netherbow Gate

clix

The Flodden Wall was not the only wall built to protect the city. Inside Flodden, several more walls were constructed as additional defenses against enemy invasion. During the 1750s, the city exploded in population, estimated to be about 50,000 people. The problem with overcrowding and a lack of sanitation systems created huge problems for the city to navigate. The solution was to build the living spaces higher. During this time, New Town had not been built, and the city was running out of room to house the number of people moving into the walled city. By the 18th century, the wall had fallen into disrepair. With no external threats, the city no longer viewed the wall as a form of protection. Instead, the wall had become a hindrance, and the city decided to build over the rubble.

World's End marks the border of the former Flodden Wall at the Netherbow Port. The port's massive gate, although no longer present today, was one of the strongest defense ports in the city. Relic remains of the stone towers can be viewed from Drummond St. and Pleasance on Forrest Rd. Today, the remains of the Flodden Wall can be seen in sections throughout the city.[clx] The Netherbow gates were torn down in 1764. The only remnant of the ancient gate is the bell tucked away in the storytelling center. [clxi]

# Blue Police Box

clxii

The long TV series Doctor Who has brought the blue police box back in popularity. The police box, while sensationalized by Doctor Who, although not technically a time machine, the blue police box has managed to survive time itself and is successfully being revitalized to adapt to the 21st century.

    The first police signal box appeared in the city of Glasgow in August 1880, and connected a line between the western and central police station, roughly 2 miles long. By 1886, the signal box expanded communication enabling the fire department and both police stations to connect the Chief Constable's House, which served as the telephone exchange point. The popularity of the police box prompted a further expansion of the police signal boxes throughout the city. In 1891, Charles Eggar patented the newer police box design, and the city of Glasgow approved the addition of the phones in the box. The signal box had two purposes: communication and shelter. The officer could place a call to the local station, but communication was a bit different when the station needed to contact the officer. The station had to send an electric current signaling a gas release to illuminate the lantern at the top of the box. At the red signal, the officer would insert a constable key to revert the signal to telephone mode before he could contact the office for instruction. After receiving the information, the officer would need to switch the box back to receiving a gas signal.[clxiii]

clxiv

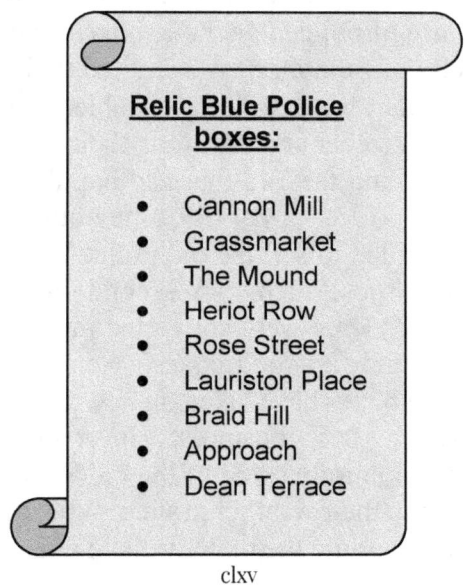

**Relic Blue Police boxes:**

- Cannon Mill
- Grassmarket
- The Mound
- Heriot Row
- Rose Street
- Lauriston Place
- Braid Hill
- Approach
- Dean Terrace

clxv

*Police phone stand 1894*

By 1930, Edinburgh had adopted the newer-designed blue police box that is commonly seen today. Inside the small blue police box, the officer had a tiny room to conduct his work in, a small sink, a kettle, and two chairs. Unlike Doctor Who's Tardis, the box was not bigger on the inside. The box served the officers well, providing them with warmth on cold winter evenings (a small oil lamp and an electric fire) and shelter on rainy days and nights. Not only did the box provide basic comforts, but it also served a second purpose as a temporary jailhouse for locals who partied a little too much. At its peak, a total of 142 were actively used throughout Edinburgh. Before the invention of the modern-day phone, police boxes were a vital source of communication between the people and the police.

With the innovation of personal radios in the 1970s, the use of police telephone boxes began to fade out. The city of Edinburgh was littered with relic blue police boxes that were no longer viable for the police department. Weather and time took their toll on the old wooden boxes and the 142 that had populated the city soon dwindled to 75.[clxvi] By 1995, the Lothian and Border Police decided to sell the old police boxes to businesses to repurpose them. A second sale was conducted in 2012. They were converted into ticket sales, coffee shops, and fast-food boxes. No longer painted royal blue, the boxes have taken on new artistic designs to promote the new business. However, sprinkled throughout Edinburgh, some of the old, derelict police boxes remain in their weathered state. Who knows, perhaps you will run into the real Tardis in your search for the old blue box.

# Moray House - 1843

clxvii

University of Edinburgh
Holyrood Road Edin-
burgh, EH8 8AQ, UK

The Moray House School of Education is often over-looked. The dark spire entrance entices passersby to wonder what this old Gothic-style building was used for. Like many structures along the Royal Mile, the Moray House is steeped in the history of the city. Beginning in 1843, the house served Canongate as a school after the Great Disruption of 1843.

During the Scottish Reformation, the Scottish people united in support for the Church of Scotland, but peaceful coexistence did not last. The root cause of the Disruption of 1843 begins with the passing of the Patronage Act in 1715. The law granted local Lairds the authority to select the ministers in their territory. The

145

members of the kirk did not have a voice in who their laird [clxviii] chose. The kirk members were not content and believed that they should be granted a vote on who became their minister.

The first secession of both ministers and members took place in the 1730s, when a group known as Seceders formed a separate church, the United Secession. The split from the Church of Scotland was primarily based on ecclesiology and ecclesiastical policy. In 1733, Stirling Minister Ebenzer Erskine resigned his post as minister, sparking a secession. This was followed by a second wave of succession in 1761 led by Thomas Gillespie. Gillespie broke from the Church of Scotland and formed his own kirk entitled the Relief Church. A movement for change was happening as local ministers and congregations were seeking to maintain a voice in their faith and leadership. The Reform Act of 1832, following the creation of the Evangelicals, became the final event that would place the Church of Scotland in a state of crisis. The Evangelicals aligned their beliefs with those of John Calvin. Inspired by Calvinist theology, the Evangelicals promoted mission-minded work throughout Scotland and overseas. These factors became the final catalyst for the Great Disruption. Religious lines were drawn between members of the Evangelical Calvinist theology and Moderates, who supported the Patronage Act. The Evangelicals opposed laird authority and pushed for the kirks to break ties with the state. By 1843, the Kirks General Assembly passed the Veto Act, authorizing the congregation to deny laird's selected minister if the majority household heads were opposed. The Veto Act was challenged by John Hope, Dean of the Faculty of Advocates. As one of Scotland's leading legal advisors,

Hope blocked the law within the court system. The Veto Act was finally decided by the House of Lords, who claimed that "the General Assembly did not have the legal right to amend the Patronage Act. " [clxix] Tensions reached a breaking point in 1842. The General Assembly drafted the Claim of Rights, which stated that the kirk did not wish for the state to interfere in the affairs of the church.

To calm the storms, several ministers gathered in Edinburgh to meet with the government. The ministers appealed to the government, stating that the kirk had no intentions of creating problems; instead, the ministers were only acting on their integrity and principles as men of God. This meeting was the minister's final attempt to come to a peaceful resolution, but the government boldly rejected the Claim of Right, since the church was seeking to overthrow the government's authority.

After the government made their stance clear, the community and the ministers began their protest, openly declaring the establishment of the Free Church of Scotland. A total of 474 ministers walked out of their churches. The ministers were suddenly homeless and broke. During this Great Disruption, the community created the Sustenion Fund, providing 150 pounds a year for the protesting ministers. Scotland now had two kirks operating in the country: the Church of Scotland and the Free Church. Soon, the Free Kirk established their own building, schools, and training programs. The Free Church had a passion for mission work, established Sunday School classes, helped with orphans and neglected children, and promoted strong theological education. The Moray House School of

147

Education was created from the Evangelical movement of the Free Church of Scotland.

## Story of the Moray House

- 1907 - Moray House joined the Church of Scotland as a training college.
- 1929 - the Free Church of Scotland reunited with the United Presbyterian Church becoming the United Free Church.
- 1965- became the Moray House of College and Education.
- 1980 - merged with Callendar Park College of Physical Education.
- 1987 - merged with the Dunfermline College of Physical Education - becoming two campuses: Holyrood and Cramond.
- 2019 - Moray House was changed to the Moray School of Education.

clxx

*Moray House Summer Garden Shed*

Holyrood Road, Edin-
burgh EH8 8BA

Located on the north side of Holyrood Rd., behind
Moray House, is a small building often mistaken for an
old shed. The Moray House Summer Garden shed
played a significant role in shaping Scotland and its relationship with the English Crown. In 1707, a very unpopular historic event took place: the Acts of Union.
This law dissolved the Scottish Parliament, making the
English Parliament the central governing body for both
England and Scotland.

Edinburgh's streets were crowded with citizens protesting the Acts of Union. As the protesters crowded the streets, the delegates were unable to enter the Scottish Parliament. The delegates made a last-minute decision to escape to a private garden behind Moray House, gathering in the little summer house at the rear. The two delegates successfully signed the Acts of Union without disruption on January 16, 1707. The passage of the Acts of Union changed Scotland forever as the law gave birth to the kingdoms of Great Britain we know today. Scotland was no longer its own country, instead it became part of the British Crown.

The small, historical building has been carefully preserved to see the place where the Acts of Union were signed. Although the story of the Moray House and the signing of the Acts of Union had been understood as an historical event, historians have recently uncovered evidence that has disproved the long-held story. According to the University of Edinburgh, "It is now thought unlikely that the Acts of Union was signed at the Moray House Summer House. Although it is possible that some signatures were added to this building. The only necessary signature would have been the Royal Assent."[clxxi] Although historical evidence fails to support the event taking place in the summer house, the tale of the Moray Summer House continues to this day.

# Canongate Kirk: 1649, 1688

clxxii

*In 1688 King James VII*
*Ordained that the Mortification of thos. (Thomas) Moodie*
*granted in 1649 to build a church should be applied to the*
*erection of this structure.*

Canongate Kirk is located near Holyrood Palace and has been frequented by royal residents during their stay in Canongate. The plaque, located above the Dutch gable, provides the original date of construction in 1649. Hung above the plaque is the crest of Thomas Moodie. The second crest, at the peak of the roof, is the crest of William III. By the time the kirk was completed in 1691, William III had displaced King James VII/II.

    Although the kirk was constructed during an era

151

of Presbyterianism, architect James Smith designed the kirk in the shape of the Roman Cross. Speculation behind Smith's design surmised that he deliberately designed the kirk so it could be easily reconverted back into a Roman Catholic church if the religious tides began to turn in Scotland.[clxxiii]

# Canongate Tolbooth Tavern-
# 1591

clxxiv

167 Canongate, Edinburgh,
EH8 8BN, UK

Canongate Tolbooth dates to 1591 and served as a dividing point between two medieval towns, the Royal Burgh of Edinburgh and Canongate burgh. The original purpose of the gate was to protect the inhabitants from undesirables entering the town, but it also served as a toll collection point. Over time, the Tolbooth expanded its use and served as the council chamber, police court, and local prison.

In contrast to Edinburgh's notorious Tolbooth prison at Canongate was not thought to be a cruel

153

prison. Instead, its inmates were mostly those who had committed infractions or failed to pay fines. One of the more notable events taking place in the Canongate Tolbooth took place in 1654, when Oliver Cromwell's troops arrested enemies of Scotland. The prisoners did not stay in the prison very long before they plotted an escape plan. They succeeded in tying their sheets together to form a rope and climbed out of the window. Another notable event happened during the Scottish Reformation (1661 - 1688) when Scottish Presbyterians, AKA Covenanters, were arrested for treason and sent to Canongate prison. The religious prisoners would not only be detained but also sent to labor camps in the Caribbean. To make matters worse, the prisoners were marked on their faces for all to see their crimes.

As wars and conflicts between England and Scotland began to calm down, peace would take the place of violence. Although unpopular among the Scots, the unification of the two countries opened a gateway for people traveling throughout the United Kingdom. Because of its closeness to Holyrood Palace, Canongate became a more popular destination for nobility seeking an escape from Edinburgh's overcrowding. The garden and orchards were favorites of the nobles residing in Canon Burgh. Despite the passing of the Union of Crowns in 1707 and the dissolution of the Scottish Parliament, Canongate remained a popular place for the nobility and professionals to live.

The tranquility of Canongate would soon change when the Act of Parliament authorized the construction of New Town in Edinburgh in 1767. The transformation of the Nor Loch into Princes Street Gardens expanded Edinburgh's footprint into Canon with the addition of the North Bridge in 1772. With Edinburgh's expansion, new technology pressed closer into Canon and marked the shift from tranquility to industrialism. The introduction of Edinburgh's gas light company brought light into the darkness of the city by 1817. The city also added a railway to transport coal from Dalkeith to Edinburgh and Glasgow. Following the railway, local industries brought manufacturing jobs to the city. In 1841, the city's population increased from 6,200 to 8,932. The distinction between Edinburgh and Canongate was dissolving at an alarming rate. By 1865, Canongate had merged into the City of Edinburgh, completing the Royal Mile we know today.[clxxv]

The Tolbooth is one of the oldest buildings harkening back to the ancient town. The transition from a prison to a tavern took place after Canongate became a part of Edinburgh. Over the years the building changed to adapt to its new role in the city. In 1884, the clock was added. To the left of the clock face is King David I's symbol of the Holyrood stag with a cross in the center of the antlers. This clock is the only reminder of the mighty gate that once stood as a barrier to those seeking entrance into the city.[clxxvi] Highlighting Canongate Tolbooth is a plaque dedicated in honor of King James. On the plaque is the national flower of Scotland, the Thistle. Reimagining the old Tolbooth into a tavern helped preserve the structure, enabling the building and its history to survive to the modern day.

Today, visitors can dine in the Tolbooth Tavern. There have been reports of supernatural events taking place inside the tavern. Incidences of falling objects and things being moved around have been heavily reported by staff and occupants. This has given rise to the tavern's reputation as being one of the most haunted buildings in Edinburgh. An old superstition claims seashells possess some type of protection that discourages the presence of harmful spirits from inhabiting the structure. Evidence of people seeking to ward off spirits is found in the exterior wall near the clock tower where seashells have been wedged in the walls.

# People's Story Museum

clxxvii

| Free admission | Canongate Tolbooth Royal Mile, Edinburgh EH8 *BN |
|---|---|

The People's Story Museum would appear to be a strange name for a museum, but the building's name comes from its remarkable collection of stories. These stories are told from the perspective of the working-class people of 18th-20th century Edinburgh. The museum houses treasures of the past, displaying items such as "tableaux, original objects, images, and personal stories to reveal their fascinating history of the city."[clxxviii] The museum's unique point is that history is told through the point of view of the people. Throughout the museum, guests can witness the culture, crafts, trades, real stories, and opinions of the everyday working class of Edinburgh citizens. Displays

157

marking key points of opposition, social political reform, and protest demonstrate the turbulent transformation of their time.

# Canongate Mercat Cross

clxxix

Along the Royal Mile toward Holyrood Palace, are two distinct sites. The first is the Mercat Cross at Canongate. In comparison to Edinburgh's Mercat Cross, which is substantially larger in size and boasts of a platform for official proclamations, the Canongate Mercat Cross is much smaller in stature and fails to capture much attention from behind metal gate poles. The size of the cross does not indicate anything, other than that the town was legally allowed to conduct business.

# Queensberry House 1667 and 1808

clxxx

64 Canongate, Edinburgh, EH8 8BZ, UK

Originally built in 1667, this 300-year-old building has its fair share of skeletons in its closet. Queensberry was founded as a grand lodge by Margaret Douglas of Balmakelly. In 1686, the lodge was sold to the 1st Duke of Queensberry to house his family in Edinburgh. Through extensive renovations, the original lodge morphed into one of the most magnificent houses in the region. According to the historic records, the house had 52 rooms, each with its own hearths. This is a dramatic improvement from the original 18-room home of Margaret Douglas. In every way, the Queensberry House boasted wealth and was held in high esteem for its contemporary architecture.

As grand as Queensberry House was, it could not hide its dark history. James Douglas Queensberry, the 3rd Marquess of Queensberry and Earl of Drumlanrig, was considered insane from birth with a reputation for having violent, chaotic behavior. The family decided to keep their disturbed son confined in the basement of the home. Two servants, aware of his behavior, were assigned to keep guard over James Douglas because he could not be left unmonitored. To make matters worse, James Douglas was not only considered aggressively insane, but he also possessed superhuman strength that could easily overpower the strongest of men.

Not many people were aware of James Douglas and his outbursts. The family had successfully kept him hidden from public view for many years. His assigned servants, tasked with watching over him, were very loyal and kept their silence about James. However, like all secrets, they have a way of coming out. On January 16, 1707, the Acts of Union was signed,[clxxxi] The house was in chaos as everyone was scurrying around preparing for the event. During the preparations, the earl was left by himself, and he made his escape from his room. During his journey, he found the kitchen and a lone kitchen servant, who was unaware of James Douglas and his turbulent behavior. Suddenly, James attacked the servant. When everyone returned to the house, an unusual smell of burnt meat brought people into the kitchen. Ten-year-old James Douglas was caught red-handed consuming the dead servant.[clxxxii]

While the story of James Douglas is horrific by itself, it is important to mention that much of the story

161

is considered speculation with no witnesses or official diagnoses. No one truly knows the extent of James Douglas' mental state or the actual events that took place in the house before people returned. Despite limited information, the story of the 'Queensberry Cannibal' became associated with the family name and their home. The family did not feel that James could take over as heir to the family, and Charles, their second son, became the family's unofficial heir. James was removed from the succession four years later. Very little is known about young James after the tragic incident. The final mention of James came in 1715, when James Douglas passed away at the age of 18 in Yorkshire, under the care of Mr. Richardson.[clxxxiii]   As for James' brother Charles, he became Privy Counsellor and Vice Admiral of Scotland. The family name continued despite the tale of the Queensberry Cannibal.

The Queensberry house has continued to play a vital role in the community. By the 18th century, the house had been redesigned into apartments housing locals. During the 19th century, the house changed from an apartment to a hospital and a barracks. In 1834, the house was transformed into a home for the poor, offering an infirmary for the sick and food for the hungry. The house nicknamed the Cannibal of Queensberry became a house to care for the poorest of society, giving them hope and security. By 1937, the House for the Poor had provided shelter for 6,627 people and fed 14,183 meals.

In 1945, the house was once again used as a hospital for the elderly. By 1997, the house was called to serve the community as the New Parliament building. Extensive renovations were needed to bring the

300-year-old building into the modern world. Surprisingly, the renovations brought the house back to its original design. Despite the skeletons in its closet, the historic Queensberry House has become intricately woven into the city of Edinburgh, meeting the needs of the challenging world around it.

# New Scottish Parliament

clxxxiv / clxxxv

Holyrood, Edinburgh,
EH99 1SP, UK

Along the way to Holyrood Palace stands an unusual,
modern building. This building is the Scotland Parliament. There is much controversy surrounding its modern design. For those who enjoy the vision of modern
buildings among a city of ancient buildings, the Parliament Building may be a fresh welcome; but others find
it hard to envision this building representing the rich
history of Edinburgh.

This building cost 400 million pounds, an
amount substantially higher than the original estimate,
and took three years longer than the original projected
date of completion. The exterior is not actually
adorned with quotation marks; instead, the architectural design was intended to resemble curtains resting
alongside the windows of the building. The message

in the design is to inform the locals that Parliament is always open to the public because the uncovered windows allow people to see inside the building all the time. Another remarkable feature on the exterior of the building are famous quotes of inspiration from Scotland's famous writers.

The front courtyard has a bizarre set of bike racks. Lined up in just the right angle, they form an image of a bike. This optical illusion is another unique feature adding to the modern design of the building.

# Abbey Sanctuary

clxxxvi

Abbey Ct House Abbey
Strand Edinburgh, EH8

While walking along the Royal Mile, people are encouraged to look up and admire the surrounding architecture." However, even the ground holds history. Scattered throughout the Royal Mile is a peculiar symbol
engraved on some of the cobblestone. Near the Queen's
Gallery and Holyrood Abbey, lies a golden-shaped letter 'S.' The golden 'S' is the sanctuary stone marking
the five-mile perimeter of the Abbey Sanctuary. The
Abbey served as a sanctuary for criminals seeking protection. If the criminal stayed within the boundaries of
the Abbey, they were safe from harm and arrest. By
the 16th century, the Crown instituted restrictions on
who qualified for protection. The king authorized
sanctuary for those who were in debt.

The debtor did not stay at the Abbey for free. They were charged rent to pay for shelter and food, but the rent was very cheap. The Abbey had established strict criteria for their sanctuary residence. From Monday to Saturday, the debtor could stay at the Abbey free of harassment. On Sunday, the debtor could leave the sanctuary without worry because it was God's Day, and no work was to be done on Sunday.[clxxxvii] Debtors seeking to stay at the Abbey beyond 24 hours had to apply for 'Bailie of the Abbey' and were given lodging in the Abbey Laird. In 1880, a law was passed that forbade the imprisonment of debtors ending the need for the Abbey's role as sanctuary of the town.[clxxxviii]

# Holyrood Palace

clxxxix

$$$ admission

Canongate, Edinburgh, EH8 8DX, UK

At the end of the Royal Mile is Holyrood Palace. The gated palace remains an active residence for the monarchy. Although Palace tours are available, sections of the royal residence remain closed to the public. When the Royalty is in residence, the Union Jack flag is flown above, and tours are not available. But when the Royalty is absent, the Rampant Lion flag is flown above, and tour-guided sessions become available.

The palace originated as the royal hunting grounds of Scottish King David I. He resided in Edinburgh Castle and walked down to the forest area to hunt deer. Legend has it that one day, King David I went hunting and encountered a deer. Whether this encounter was physical or mere vision is debated. The true origin of this story has been lost in time. In the vision, the king saw a cross hovering above the deer's head between the antlers. King David was deeply religious, and believed that the sign was from God, telling him to build an abbey on the site.

The abbey was named Holyrood Abbey, translated as Holy Cross, in honor of the King's vision of the image of the deer and the cross he saw on that day. Construction of the Abbey began in 1128. As time passed, visiting monarchs would stay at the Abbey, often for extended periods of time. Over the years, additional rooms and buildings were added to adapt to the royal visitors.

By 1500, the Abbey had been transformed into a nice vacation home for the royals. Eventually, the decision was made to change the Abbey to a royal palace because the convenience and modernity of the Abbey were preferred overstaying at Edinburgh Castle.[cxc]

Mary, Queen of Scots was a frequent visitor to Holyrood Palace during her reign. Within the palace walls is a special room that remains to the present day, where Mary, Queen of Scots, stayed. A story about an ill-fated night at the palace sealed itself in history and is often retold to visitors.

On March 9th, 1566, at 8pm the 4th Earl of Morton, Lord Ruthven, Lord Darnley, Queen Mary's second husband, led 80 men to the queen's supper chamber. Mary, who was six months pregnant at the time, was having a delightful meal with David Riccio, the queen's secretary, and her handmaiden. Suddenly, Lord Darnley stormed into the room, followed by Lord

Ruthven. The men informed the queen that Riccio had been accused of offending her honor. Mary told them that the accusation about Riccio would be dealt with by the Lord of Parliament, but this did not satisfy her husband. Darnley told Ruthven to restrain the queen as he dealt with Riccio himself. The frightened Riccio hid behind the queen for protection. Mary was infuriated but unable to do anything while held at gunpoint. The assassins grabbed Riccio and proceeded to attack him with knives. After an estimated 56 knife wounds, Riccio perished; his lifeless body was thrown down the stairs. After Riccio's death, the assassins fled the palace, fearing retribution from the queen. No longer at gunpoint, Mary confronted her husband. Darnley claimed that he was told that she was having an affair with Riccio. Darnley blamed Riccio for the problems they were having in their marriage, even suggesting that the baby may not be his. After her husband left, Darnley ordered sentries to remain outside of her door preventing her from leaving the Palace. She managed to conspire a plan to escape.[cxci] She succeeded in "beguiling him (Lord Darnley) with soothing words," persuading him to escape to Dunbar Castle with her, with help from the Earl of Boswell. [cxcii]

During Mary's rule in Scotland, the country was predominantly Protestant, led by Calvinist John Knox. The queen was Catholic. The animosity between the two religious groups pitted Protestant Scottish nobles against the queen. The plot to attack Riccio was spurred by nobles fearing the upcoming parliament session, in which Mary planned to forfeit the property of Lords who had rebelled against her during Chaseabout Raid. Lord Darnley's role in the assassination of

Riccio was under false pretenses. The rebellious nobles had successfully convinced Darnley that his wife was having an affair with Riccio and the heir to the throne was not his. This spurred her husband to act against his wife and participate in the murder of her secretary.

## Chaseabout Raid 1565

The rebellion led by James Stuart, 1st Earl of Moray against his half-sister Mary Queen of Scots in March of 1565, protesting the queen's marriage to Lord Darnley. It was never an actual battle, rather it was a rebellion that pitted Mary's superior forces of 5,000 against the noble rebels. The rebels would frequently move back and forth between England and Scotland, known as the Chase-about-Raid to avoid direct battle with the queen's troops. The rebellion reached its conclusion when the group arrived in Edinburgh, and realized there was little support for their cause, failing to elicit the needed men to stand against the queen.

Problems against Mary began in the noble's opposition against the Queen's marriage, July 29, 1565, to Lord Darnley. Henry Stuart led by protestant Earl of Moray, an unofficially supported by Queen Elizabeth II. The Scottish nobles feared the Catholic marriage would threaten the Protestant Reformation that had grown in Scotland, during Mary's absence to her first husband, the Dauphin of France on April 24, 1558. In 1559, the newlyweds became the new rulers of France, after the sudden death of King Henry II of France. Shortly after King Francis II became king, he died on December 5, 1560. No longer the Queen of France, she moved back to Scotland and reigned as a Catholic queen in a dominant Protestant country.

Despite the opposition to her, Mary would not back down in maintaining her rule in Scotland. With rumors challenging her baby's legitimacy, spurred by noble opposition, she would not be deterred from declaring her child the legitimate heir to the throne, and validate the true father of the baby. Mary wanted to deliver her son to Edinburgh Castle to secure her royal line, making her baby eligible to rule both England and Scotland, but she was aware of those who opposed her rule. Mary arrived in Edinburgh, on March 18th, 1566, with 3-5,000 troops ready to vanquish her enemies. Her rivaling nobles witnessed the queen's troops, prompting her conspirators to quickly flee to England to escape her wrath. No battles were fought, and a few days later she entered Edinburgh Castle to deliver her son James VI on June 19, 1566.[cxciii]

The nearly thousand-year-old palace is filled with the history of Scotland. For instance, Oliver Cromwell's army occupied the Palace during the English Civil War. While there, his troops destroyed large portions of the palace. This led to major restoration efforts to repair and modernize the palace in 1671. King George V played a role in bringing the palace into the 20th century by incorporating modern conveniences such as indoor heat, electricity, indoor plumbing and bathrooms, kitchen appliances, and elevators. Scottish architect Sir William Bruce designed the renovations in the palace. Today, the palace has 289 rooms including a King's Chamber and Mary, Queen of Scots' bedroom.

Before the passing of Queen Elizabeth II, it was traditional for the Queen to visit her favorite palace in Edinburgh. Every summer, around late June, and early July, she would venture to the palace. This time became known as Holyrood Week. Extravagant parties were thrown in honor of the queen's arrival.

# Lesser-Known Statues

cxciv

*Helen Acquroff Fountain Memorial is in the Meadows. It was created to remember Helen, a blind pianist who participated in the Temperance Movement.*

cxcv

*Bum the dog, a three-legged Spaniel mixed stowaway, boarded a ship from Edinburgh, Scotland bound for San Diego, California in 1886. He became the town dog in the United States. He would be seen playing with the local children and giving the kids free rides through town. His statue is located on Princes Street Garden and was given to Edinburgh as an exchange for a statue of Greyfriars Bobby in 2008.*

174

cxcvi

*David Balfour and Alan Breck Stewart statues commemorate the completion of Robert Louis Stevenson's book "Kidnapped," with the two main characters completing their journey from Corstorphine Hill to Edinburgh.*

cxcvii

*The Great Lafayette, famed magician, loved his dog Beauty to an extreme. He pampered her with expensive beads, collars, and food. It is said Lafayette fed her to death. In truth Beauty was 15 years old when she passed. After her death on May 4, 1910, Lafayette decided to be buried with her when he died.*

175

cxcviii

*Elsie Inglis Memorial Plaque is dedicated to a female doctor who fought during the Suffrage Movement and pushed for women to be allowed to attend Edinburgh University*

cxcix

*Sir Walter Scott, known for his talented writings of the Waverly Novels, had a loyal companion named Maida, a wolf deerhound cross. She was often depicted at the feet of her owner in portraits.*

cc

*James Clerk Maxwell, famed physicist, found that he enjoyed the company of animals over people. Toby, an Irish Terrier, became his constant companion. Maxwell would often discuss his theories and discoveries with Toby. One fascination of Maxwell's was the study of color blindness. He used Toby as his study case, using his crudely made ophthalmoscope to examine his dog's eyes to aid him in his interest in the rare genetic disorder.*

cci

*Robert Fergusson, famed poet, is known for his poem, 'Auld Reekie.' The young poet was met with a sad end when had taken a fall down a staircase at the age of 24 yrs. (1774). While he survived, he was declared mentally ill from his injuries. Attempts were made to create a hospital to care for mentally ill patients but there was little success in raising the necessary funds. Robert Fergusson was unable to receive the care he needed. Eighteen years after his passing, funds were provided in Fergusson's honor to build the Andrew Duncan Royal Edinburgh Hospital for Neuro-Behavioral Rehabilitation Service Unit was completed in honor of Robert Fergusson.*

ccii

*Veteran Memorial at Canongate on the Royal Mile*

# Greyfriars Bobby Statue

cciii

Candlemaker Row, Edinburgh, EH1 1QE, UK

A dog is a man's best friend.' This short phrase has captured the hearts of many who have heart-felt stories about their faithful companion. Greyfriar Bobby's canine tale features his faithful loyalty to his beloved master. The story of Bobby was so remarkable that a statue of the Skye Terrier was made in honor of his loyalty to his owner.

Out of all the dog stories in the world, what is so significant about Greyfriars Bobby? The story of Bobby takes place in the mid-1800s, when a night watchman, Constable No. 90, named John Gray, adopted a young Skye Terrier to be his working companion. As a result, the town came to associate Bobby with Constable Gray. However, Bobby's world suddenly came to an abrupt halt. On February 15, 1858, his owner passed away from tuberculosis. Constable John Gray was buried in the local cemetery at Greyfriars Kirkyard.

cciv

*Bobby*

Bobby was left without his owner, but he re-fused to leave his master. Days after the passing of Grey, Bobby was spotted laying over the grave of his owner. The caretaker attempted to remove Bobby, and Grey's family tried to bring the dog back home, but to no avail. Bobby refused any effort to relocate him from his owner. Despite having no master, Bobby continued the same schedule he and John Grey had done for years. At 1 p.m., castle guns would fire, and Bobby would stop by his favorite restaurant to get a bite to eat. The restaurant owner was a friend of John's and had often given Bobby food when the constable stopped by. The passing of John Grey did not stop Bobby from contin-uing the same route he and his owner had taken. Soon, local support for Bobby grew, and the story of Greyfri-ars Bobby began to spread beyond the town.

In 1867, a new law was passed that required all dogs to have a city tag, or the dog would be euthanized.

Lord Provost paid for Bobby to have a city tag and presented the faithful dog with a collar embossed with the inscription, "Greyfriars Bobby from the Lord Provost 1867."[ccv] Bobby passed away at the age of 16 in 1872. The tale of the dog's extreme loyalty, even in death, spread further beyond the borders of Scotland and captured the attention of London's philanthropist, Baroness Angelia Georgina Burdett-Coutts, President of the Ladies Committee of the RSPCA. The story of Bobby deeply affected the baroness, and she asked the city government if she could donate her own money to have a granite fountain with a bronze statue of Bobby. With the local popularity of Bobby, the council granted the baroness's request. William Brody, a local sculptor, set to work creating the statue of Bobby by 1873, a year after the passing of the Skye terrier. The Greyfriars Bobby statue was erected at the corner of George IV Bridge and Candlemaker Row, opposite the graveyard where John Grey was buried. On the statue, Bobby's affection for his owner is displayed for all to see on a plaque reading, "A tribute to an affectionate fidelity of Greyfriars Bobby."[ccvi]

The statue was originally a fountain with two bowls. The top bowl was for people and the lower bowl was for dogs to drink from. Over time, the fountain disappeared, and what remains is the Greyfriars Bobby statue. Visitors and locals still try to remember and pay their respect for little Bobby in his passing. Visitors affectionately rub the nose of the statue as they pass by, for good luck, like one would rub the nose of their pet. The years of nose rubs have taken a toll on the statue. Signs to encourage people to resist rubbing Bobby's nose have been posted to preserve the statue, but many passing by find it difficult to resist the urge to do so.

As a result, Bobby has had to undergo two nose replacements over the years, costing nearly £400 in 2014. In 2018, a campaign to 'Save Bobby's Nose' was used to encourage awareness through Facebook, and finally, decisions were made to create a barrier around Bobby to further preserve his nose.

The story of Bobby and his extreme loyalty to his master, John Grey, has captured the hearts of people around the world. In 2015, Deidre Brock, Depute Lord Provost, hosted an event to honor Bobby. The memorial states, "Let his loyalty and devotion be a lesson to us all; 'he still inspires enormous affection and respect in people across the globe."[ccvii] Bobby's fame has spread throughout the world, and he continues to inspire visitors with his affection and loyalty.

# 1ˢᵗ Duke Wellington

ccviii

9 Waterloo Pl, Edinburgh,
EH1 3BG, UK

Located in front of the Register House is a statue of Arthur Wellesley, the 1st Duke of Wellington. He was born in Dublin, Ireland. Although the Duke was not native-born, he had many military and political accomplishments that played a significant role in history to justify his memorialization as a statue in Edinburgh. ccix

### Duke of Wellington:

- 1793-1802 Fought in the French Revolution
- 1796-served in India became chief advisor to Nizam of Hyderabad's army
- 1802-became major-general in the 2nd Maratha Wars (1803-1805)
- 1803-claimed victory in Assaye

- 1806-became a Tory in English Parliament
- 1807- served in Copenhagen, Denmark
- 1808-became Lieutenant General after defeat of the French at Rolica and Vimeiro, Portugal
- Developed his famous French Column with reverse twist slope defense strategy.
- 1809-claimed victory at Talavera.
- 1811-defeated the French at Fuentes de Onoro
- 1812-claimed Ciudad Rodrigo
- 1813-destroyed the French army at Vittoria, Spain
- 1815-claimed victory in the Battle of Waterloo
- 1828-1839 & 1834-Served as Prime minister for the Tories.
- 1829-oversaw the passing of the Catholic Emancipation
- 1832-he opposed the Reform Act.

He is remembered more for his military contributions than his political career. In 1842, John Steell was commissioned by the city of Edinburgh to construct a statue of the 1st Duke of Wellington. Steell captured one of the greatest moments of the duke's life during the Battle of Waterloo in 1815 and included the duke's favorite horse, Copenhagen. The sculpture depicts Wellington riding astride Copenhagen with calm assurance as he led the campaign to defeat Napoleon. His victory guaranteed freedom for England and the European countries. Funding for the sculpture came through the donations of landowners, political opponents, and Tories.[ccx] By 1852, the duke's iron statue was unveiled. The statue represents the military accomplishments of an Irish man who fought in the Napoleonic Wars and defeated Napoleon in the Battle of Waterloo.

# Calton Hill

ccxi

Free admission

32 Greenside rd., Edinburgh
& Lothians, EH1 3AJ, UK

Purchased by the town council of Edinburgh in 1724, Calton Hill, resting on an extinct volcano, is one of the oldest public parks in Britain. The town council had planned to use the park as part of their efforts to create national monuments for the town to celebrate the famous Scotsman Burns Monument, Nelson's Monument, and David Hume's walk.

Scotland's famous philosopher David Hume was an advocate of ensuring the health and well-being of the citizens of the town. He campaigned for the town council to create a walking path for the townspeople to walk in the open, fresh air, removed from Auld Reekie. The town council granted his request in 1775, a year prior to Hume's passing.

Hume's love for Calton Hill overflowed into his last wishes when he asked to be buried "in a private manner in the Calton Hill Churchyard and a monument built over his body, not exceeding 100 pounds."[ccxii] The town of Edinburgh honored his last request and had his tombstone placed in Calton Burial Grounds at the base of Calton Hill. Today, the walkway is called Humes Walk.

ccxiii

*Pantheon of Athens*

Calton Hill is filled with monuments celebrating Scotland's history. One monument, known as Edinburgh's 'Shame, is the unfinished National Monument of Scotland: The Acropolis. Construction began in 1816, marking the end of Napoleon's defeat at Waterloo (1803-1815). The monument was designed to replicate the Parthenon in Athens. Edinburgh was experiencing a season of intellectual brilliance in architecture (1816-1829) and the Greek Neoclassical style

187

was popular at the time, so naturally, the city embraced the design of the Pantheon to serve as the national monument of Scotland. Unfortunately, the passion for the style did not extend enough to pay for the complete construction of the monument. Funds quickly dried up in 1829, and the monument remains incomplete. Visitors can only imagine what the completed form would have been. Known as the National Disgrace of Scotland, the column monument remains a reminder of Edinburgh's failed attempt to finish what they began over 100 years ago.[ccxiv]

ccxv/ccxvi

*(left side) Nelson's Monuments, (right side) Observatory*

One of the tallest monuments erected perpendicular on Calton's Hill is Nelson's Monument. The monument honors Vice Admiral Horatio Nelson's success in the Battle of Trafalgar in 1805 during the Napoleonic Wars. The battle was a success for Britain, although Nelson perished during his moment of triumph. News quickly spread to Edinburgh of Nelson's victory and sacrifice. Funds were quickly gathered to construct a monument in his honor. Robert Burns petitioned to design the monument as an upturned telescope. Construction began in 1807, but due to a delay in funding the full cost of the project, the monument was not completed until 1816. In the meantime, unique efforts were made to generate the necessary funds. Ideas such as charging a small entrance fee to enter the tower and charging ex-sailors a small fee to rent the building helped to offset the cost, but the final solution was more inventive. It was presented by the widow of a petty officer who had moved into the monument. She established a restaurant selling soups, jellies, breakfast, coffee, and tea to the locals. Her efforts provided enough funds to complete the construction of the Nelson Monument. Although setting up a restaurant may seem strange, this was not the only bizarre event that took place at Nelson's Monument. A visitor from Lapland (Scandinavians known as the Sami people) took his reindeer to the top of the monument in 1822 as a publicity stunt.[ccxvii]

Nelson is known as the greatest officer in the history of the Royal Navy. The monument is 30 meters tall, and the tower houses 147 steps. At the top of the monument is a white cross. In addition to honoring Nelson, the Telescope Tower has a time ball, installed in 1852, located at the top of the tower. Professor Charles Piazzi Smith, a Royal Astronomer from Scotland, suggested that the tower aide ships at sea. The idea was that "the ball would drop at exactly 1 p.m., as a signal to ships moored in the Firth of Forth, enabling captains to check the accuracy of their chronometer and correctly calculate their longitude at sea."[ccxviii] While the idea was sound, the application was flawed. Initially, the plan was for the ball to function as the signal, but Edinburgh's thick fog made it difficult to see the visual signal. The second option was to use sound. This solution was created to correct the limited visibility produced by the fog, which prevented the sailors from coordinating their chronometers at sea. In 1861, when the 1pm gun blast from Edinburgh Castle became synced with the ball drop from Nelson's Monument, an accurate time was established. To connect the two signals together, a wire was run through the city to allow the gun and ball to go off two times per day. In 2009, the Nelson Monument's Time Ball was protected by the City of Edinburgh Council and the Edinburgh World Heritage Group. Today, the need for the gunfire ball drop is no longer necessary for sea captains and it remains only for tradition for the locals and visitors to enjoy.

ccxix

### *Time at Sea*
*Sailors used chronometers to pinpoint their exact location at sea. Time has always been important to mariners, not only for scheduling timetables, but for navigating away from land. To find longitude at sea, sailors compared the local time aboard ship with time from a chronometer. Edinburgh's time-ball and time-gun enabled every ship's crew to check their chronometer before leaving port.*
### *Bang in the Middle of Edinburgh*

*The Time-Ball was invisible on foggy days, so an audible time signal was introduced in 1861 - the One O'clock Gun. The gun was located at the castle and connected to the Time-Ball by an electric wire which hung over the city. This system was so successful it later became part of a larger network of clocks around Edinburgh and was even connected electrically to time-guns in Dundee and Newcastle.*

The City Observatory was built in 1818 by William Henry Playfair. His Tuscan, Doric pedimented pavilion was shaped in the design of a Greek Cross, with "each wing having two pilastered bays and a hexastyle portico."[ccxx] Within the center of the building is the famed octagonal drum. Playfair envisioned the observatory to resemble the Temple of the Winds in Athens and Tycho Brahe's Observatory on Hven.[ccxxi] The Observatory was considered second to that of the Greenwich Observatory in London. The dome had the ability to rotate in all directions.

The Observatory clock maintained its accuracy by aligning the telescope along the meridian line. In 1854, when the Time Ball was added to the Nelson Monument, the Observatory clock controlled the timing with an electrical pulse.

The Observation Dome closed in 1930, and over the years, age and weather took its toll on the building. By the 20th century, the building was tagged as high-risk due to excessive damage to the roof from years of leaks and dry rot. A grant given by the Edinburgh World Heritage Conservation Fund Program helped to jumpstart efforts to save the building from further damage in 2014. Soon additional funds were raised and provided to continue restoration efforts. The total cost of repairs added up to 4.5 million pounds.

Four years later, the observatory was restored, and the City Observatory is once again opened for visitors to see.

# Old Calton Cemetery

ccxxii

> Free admission

> 29 Waterloo Pl, Edinburgh,
> EH1 3BG, UK

A surprise rests in the Old Calton Cemetery. In the middle of the cemetery lies a statue of Abraham Lincoln. During the American Civil War, the United States' northern and southern states were at war over the issues of sovereignty and slavery. The American Civil War was a war generally isolated from world affairs, but it did catch the eye of many nations as the world watched the internal war within the young nation's fight against

193

slavery. The fight to end slavery in the United States captured the attention of five young Scotsmen who felt compelled to fight against injustice. The valiant effort of the five Scotsmen to participate in a foreign war aboard was noble, but sadly, the men failed to return to their homeland, perishing in the war.

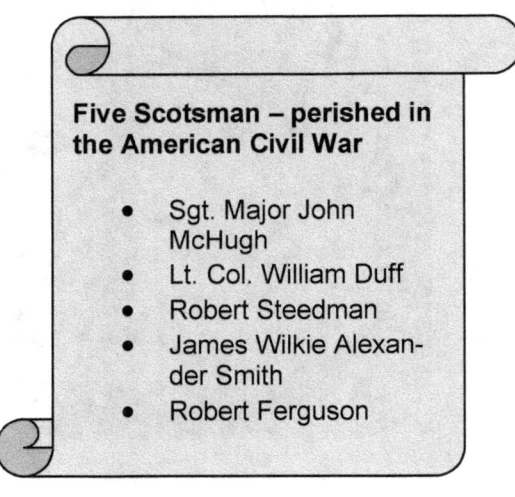

**Five Scotsman – perished in the American Civil War**

- Sgt. Major John McHugh
- Lt. Col. William Duff
- Robert Steedman
- James Wilkie Alexander Smith
- Robert Ferguson

Faced with the loss of her husband and impoverishment, Lt. Col. William McHugh's wife petitioned the United States for her husband's war pension. She struggled to obtain the needed funds to support her family, and being a foreigner, it proved harder for Ms. McHugh to plead her case in the United States. In a desperate attempt to obtain what was owed to her, she consulted US Counsel Wallace Burns for help in gaining her husband's pension. Soon, her story became public and elicited support from many in the United States. One man heard about the five Scottish volunteers and decided to erect a war memorial in honor of the Scottish men who fought in the American Civil

194

War. John D. Rockefeller personally paid the cost for the statue of Abraham Lincoln to be commissioned. Upon the statue is the American flag draped at the base of Lincoln's feet, ladened with thistles and cotton. Both images symbolize the unity of the five Scottish men and their sacrifice for the freedom of slaves in America. The statue was created in the United States and sent to Scotland in 1893, where it rests as a memorial to the brave men of Scotland.[ccxxiii]

# Edinburgh Center Bollard

ccxxiv

> 2-4 Waterloo Pl, Edinburgh,
> EH1 3EG, UK

Many people walking along Princes Street would not take a second glance at this nondescript black bollard sitting on the sidewalk. The bollard does not have a plaque or description identifying what it is or the historic significance it has in the history of Edinburgh. The short bollard could be mistaken for an old horse tie poll, but this simple black bollard is so much more than a horse tie; rather, it holds geographical significance.

The black bollard is a marker of the first Edinburgh General Post Office, and all postal codes begin at this location. In addition, the marker was used as a

196

gauge to determine the distance from one point in the city to the other locations. The street address and numbers "begin at the end of the street that's closest to the bollard"[ccxxv] and are still being used for the same purpose today. When passing by the small black marker, take some time to recognize the little black bollard's significance in the history of Edinburgh and its importance to the modern 21st century.

# Edinburgh's Dungeon

ccxxvi

$$$ admission

31 Market Street, Edinburgh, EH1 1DF, UK

Every castle has its dungeons full of mystery and horror. Oftentimes, a Dungeon tour talks about the darker side of castle life and all the horrific things that took place in the basement of the castle. Unfortunately, Edinburgh Castle Dungeon is not one of those places that offer tour, but an offsite location presents a live action demonstration of the shadowy life of castle dungeons but also brings the history to life. The sinister activities that occurred in the Edinburgh Dungeon are often left out of modern books.

198

The award-winning Edinburgh Dungeon Tours explores 1,000 years of history. The tour witnesses' history through live actors retelling the stories of William Wallace. The spooky and exciting journey will expose visitors to ancient history through the eyes of the historic figures represented. With Scottish rogues, serial killers, and the reenactments of Burke & Hare, Agnes Finnie, and Sawney Bean's family; the Edinburgh Dungeon Tours are not for the faint of heart or for young children.[ccxxvii] The life-action experience covers the court room, torture chamber, the anatomy theatre, castle ghost, and the witch trials.

The one-hour adventure tour continues to engage the visitors as they venture into 16th-century Bean Clan life. This part of the tour is a fully sensory experience where guests experience the noxious smells of the clan lair and discover remains of past visitors. It is highly recommended to make a tour reservation in advance, as the popularity of the historic adventure can quickly be filled by visitors and locals seeking a thrilling experience of Edinburgh's hidden, darker past.

# Physics Garden

ccxxviii

| Free admission | Platform 11, Waverly Station, Edinburgh EH1 1BB Scotland |
|---|---|

It can be hard to imagine a place with a name like "Physics Garden" being a popular tourist site. Back in 1670, two prominent physicians, Dr. Andrew Balfour and Dr. Robert Sibbald, shared a passion for botany. Together, the two men purchased a small section of land near Holyrood Palace. With their land, they cultivated a garden of local and foreign plants to create an apothecary garden for their patients' needs. Over the years the popularity of the plants, herbs, and flowers that had grown attracted the attention of the elite in society, who sought the clean, peaceful environment the garden offered. These two factors set the garden apart and it became a favorite place for the city of Edinburgh.

Five years after Dr. Balfour and Dr. Sibbald purchased the land, Dr. Sibbald petitioned the University of Edinburgh to grant additional funds to expand the garden based upon its growing popularity within the city. The university agreed to fund the purchase and lease of lands near Nor Loch. The Physics Garden's success allowed it to survive during industrialization. In 1763, the garden relocated to a larger, greener field near Leith, where it now stands in Haddington Place, to escape the overcrowding and influx of businesses.[ccxxix]

Today, the Physics Garden was once again moved in 1820, to Inverleigh. The move took over three years due to the care taken to preserve the large collection of plants that had grown. Over the years, the garden was expanded, and glass houses were added (1834-1858) to help tropical plants survive the harsh Scottish weather. Today, the Physics Garden boasts 70 acres and houses over 13,000 plant species.

Hidden away in the heart of Congleton is a small Georgian bath house. The bath house was owned by Bradshaw House on Lawton St., dating back to 1820. The bathhouse shares the property with a neo-classical inspired garden shed. Both buildings were annexed into the Physics Garden after the garden was relocated to its new location of Inverleigh. As with many buildings, time took its toll on both structures. By the 20th century, the Congleton Building Preservation Trust came to the rescue, securing ownership of the property. The bathhouse and shed were saved with donated funds.

Every September, the Physics Garden holds its annual Heritage Day, welcoming visitors to tour the gardens and walk through the grounds. No fee is charged to guests, but donations are appreciated. All funds are used to help maintain the gardens and structures on the property.

# Unique Places to Visit

| UK 197 Canongate Edinburgh EH8 8BN |
|---|

| $$$ store purchase |
|---|

| 30 High St., Edinburgh EH1 1TB, UK |
|---|

Walking along the Royal Mile can be like walking through time, but history is not the only selling point to attract visitors from all over the world. Along the Mile is an array of pubs, restaurants, and shops to delight all who come to see the city. Often overshadowed by the more popular tourist sites, there are local favorites. The Fudge House and Fudge Kitchen are two of these hidden gems. They aren't old businesses, just modern shops housed in old buildings. The two shops are unique and invite people to view the fudge-making process. Both locations open their doors and let people view the whole process of fudge-making. Visitors can view the skill and craft that goes into making the fudge sold in the stores. The fudge masters are available to answer questions. This is a fun experience for all ages.

ccxxx

| $$$ admission | Edinburgh, EH2 4AH, UK |

Another unassuming place to stop by and purchase a local treat is the Chocolatorium. The Chocolatorium is a separate entity from the two fudge shops that takes 90-minute tours of the facility. The Chocolatorium offers an immersive experience in the art of chocolate. Throughout the hour and a half tour, visitors can sample 40 different types of chocolate (in the tasting room) and create their own delicious treat to savor. The shop also offers some rather interesting chocolate, like Haggis Chocolate, to anyone who dares to try.

Located on Cranston St. the small chocolate factory adds a little extra to visitors' experience in the world of chocolate. It's a favorite for all ages, and a nice break from a long day of walking around and exploring Edinburgh. Prices vary and it is advisable to check the website to make reservations before heading to the Royal Mile. The Chocolatorium also has a chocolate kitchen where customers can purchase chocolate without participating in the 90-minute tour.

# Cows at Cowgate

ccxxxi

*(left side) Cows head at Cowgate St. and (right side) Cow's tail at Toon Coocilor St.*

Free admission

Cowgate(front) NT2673 & The Toon Coocillor NT2673, UK

Only in Edinburgh! Perched high above one side of the building on Cowgate and Toon Coocilor is a rather unusual-looking structure. On the wall facing Cowgate, the front portion of a cow hangs midway up the building, and the back portion hangs from the wall facing Toon Coocilor Street. The first thought that comes to mind is, why? Could it be that this bizarre split cow hints at a mind-boggling story about an incident involving a cow and the building? The stories along the Royal Mile are interesting and can seem inconceivable at times, but the split cow takes things to the next level.

Fortunately, the split cow does not hint at a tragic accident; instead, the split cow statue serves as a reminder of the history of the city. Back in the early

1400s, the town of Edinburgh was a lot smaller than it is today. As an agrarian-based society, with a trade-based economy, farmers would transport their cattle to the town for market days. Cowgate was the primary route farmers herded their cattle through, hence its namesake. This was also the period when the town had built the North and South bridges. The wealthier class would travel along the bridges to avoid the filth below, and the cows would be herded below the bridge. As the city grew, cowgate was no longer used as an entrance for cattle, instead, the impoverished, poor, beggars, and criminals began to occupy the lower ground levels of the street. Cowgate, among other streets, became defined as the slum region in Edinburgh. As the elites moved to New Town, the Old Town crime ran rampant throughout the old section of town, becoming too dangerous to journey to.

Over time and with great effort, the slums of the Old Town began to rejuvenate. Efforts to clean up the older parts of the city promoted new commerce returning to the area once again. Old Town is no longer associated with the slums and has become a popular site for locals and visitors to frequent. The split cow statue hanging on the building sides has become a town icon, with various owners adding their artistic flair to decorate the cow adorning the building over the years. Though bizarre, the cow is a reminder of the history of Cowgate and the transformation that had taken place as the city transitioned into modern times.

# St. Culbert Kirkyard

ccxxxii

Free admission

Edinburgh, EH2 4AH, UK

Located on the west end of Prince Street is Culbert's Kirkyard, an old grave site dating back to the early history of the city. Throughout the kirkyard, short towers are posted next to the graves. These towers seem out of place in the graveyard, but their story reveals a more sinister side of Edinburgh's history.

The Scottish Enlightenment began in Edinburgh in the 1800s. During this time, the medical field began to shift away from medical treatment based upon herbs and superstition to a scientific approach to treating patients. The new scientific method brought professionalism to the medical field and new students were eager to learn medicine through an enlightened lens. The University of Edinburgh's medical department needed cadavers for the students to learn about the functions of the human body, but cadavers were not easy to obtain. Strict laws were in place, limiting the types of cadavers used for science. Only criminal convicts and those executed under the law were allowed to undergo scientific dissection. Unfortunately for the universities, the demand for human cadavers far exceeded the supply of executed criminals available.

Where there is a demand, people will find a way to fill the lack of supply for a profit. A group of people realized that they could profit from deceased bodies in the church's graveyard. During the night, these people would sneak into Edinburgh graveyards, dig up fresh graves, and sell the bodies to the university for 10 shillings (for higher-quality cadavers). The pay was equal to the wage earned for 3 to 4 weeks of work. The university was desperate to provide for the medical students and turned a blind eye to how the cadavers were obtained. The graverobbers increased in number and skill, causing the townspeople to demand the city protect their dead loved ones. In response, the government-built watchtowers and hired watchmen to keep guard over the graveyards at night. Initially, the plan worked, and the number of grave robbers decreased. But the graverobbers bribed the watchmen to not report their activity, and to alert them when a new body was buried.

Between 1827 and 1828, two men, William Burke and William Hare hatched a plan to obtain bodies by luring their victim to their home. Once the victim arrived, Burke and Hare would kill the person, and sell the body to Dr. Knox. Dr. Knox was a well-known professor who eagerly paid for the bodies without questioning how Burke and Hare obtained them. Burke and Hare sold between 16 to 30 bodies to Dr. Knox within a year's time. Their greed became their downfall, and they were caught on November 1, 1828.

During the trial, Hare testified against his partner, in exchange for his freedom. Burke was proclaimed guilty and sentenced to hang on January 29, 1829. The judge also ordered that Burke's body was to be used for dissection at Edinburgh University. Burke's dissection became the most popular lecture in the history of the university. Today, Burke's skeleton is displayed in the History of Surgery and Dentistry in the Scottish Museum. Located next to his skeleton is a purse made from Burke's butt skin.[ccxxxiii] Hare was exiled from Scotland and relocated to England. He was never heard from again. Although Dr. Knox was never convicted of any crimes, his reputation was ruined, and he was forced to move to London. .[ccxxxiv]

The season of grave robbing came to an end in 1832 with the passing of the Anatomy Act.[ccxxxv] The new law allowed doctors and their students to dissect any deceased body that had been unclaimed after death (often people who had died in jail or in workhouses). The schools were no longer limited in trying to find bodies for dissection but had an influx of unclaimed bodies available.

# The Georgian House

ccxxxvi

$$$ admission

7 Charlotte Sq., Edinburgh.
Lothian, Scotland, EH2 4DR

Europe was undergoing the Industrial Revolution in the eighteenth century. Cities were upgrading and adopting new technology. The Industrial Revolution brought modernization, and Edinburgh did not want to fall behind the rest of the world. Economic concerns plagued the city and the council hoped that a new addition to the medieval city would encourage the intellectuals and wealthy elites to stay in Edinburgh.

210

The town council envisioned the new expansion to reflect the Scottish Enlightenment and offer a place where philosophers, scientists, and bold thinkers could lead the ancient city into the 18th century. The old cliche, 'build it and they will come,' became the mantra of the day. Furthermore, the council hoped residents who had left would come back to take part in the revitalization effort to transform Edinburgh for the next century. The town council decided to hold an architectural competition to find a new designer to create New Town.

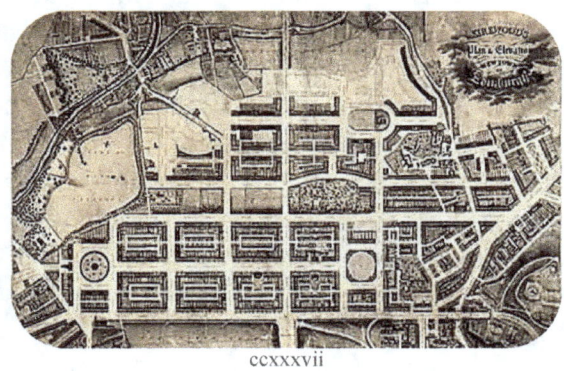

ccxxxvii

*1819 map of Edinburgh*

The competition proved to be the winning factor in helping revitalize Edinburgh. The winner was 26-year-old James Craig. He specialized in town planning and urban architecture, and his simplistic designs captured the attention of the council. Craig's design depicted a centralized street with two gardens joining the Old Town and New Town. Craig's vision was to knit both New Town and Old Town together by connecting streets running perpendicular from north to south. He chose street names that evoked patriotic pride. Under the rule of King George III, Craig chose the names: George Street and Queens Street, with their respective gardens also reflecting the royal family. One Park was called Charlotte Square, named after the Queen. The decision for the second garden's name was challenging. Many people wanted to name the park after Edinburgh's patron St. Giles. However, this was controversial since St. Giles was also the patron saint of lepers. In the end, King George decided to name the gardens after his two sons: Princes Street Gardens.[ccxxxviii]

New Town became a success, bringing prosperity back to Edinburgh. With the arrival of new residences in New Town, homes were constructed to reflect the finest of the Georgian style. Robert Adams was the visionary designer behind the New Town residences. Adams used chinoiserie influences to complete his vision for the homes he designed. Chinoiserie[ccxxxix] was popular design technique used during the 17th to 18th centuries.

The Georgian House, located near Charlotte Square, was one such house designed by Robert Adams. John Lamont, Chief of Clan Lamont, built the Georgian House and moved in. In 1815, he sold his home, and the town house passed through several Scottish families over the years. Toward the end of the 18th century, the house was purchased by the National Trust of Scotland in 1966 after its final owner, the 5th Duke Marquess of Brute, passed. The National Trust of Scotland took on the ambitious task of restoring the old home to its former elegance. Today, visitors can walk through the Georgian-style home and imagine life in the 18th-century.

This is a must-see for visitors to experience the life of the wealthy class of the 18th century. Elegance at its best is reflected throughout the home and kitchen below. To see Gladstones Landing, reflecting life in Old Town Edinburgh and the Georgian House in New Town, reflecting life in the 18th century, visitors benefit in witnessing life from two different periods in Edinburgh's history. The significant alteration in living circumstances reflects the town council's grand strategy to both modernize and conserve Edinburgh's historic core in the eighteenth century.

# Miniature Lighthouse

ccxl

Admission Free | 84 George St., Edinburgh Scotland

Along the Royal Mile, it is easy to see the numerous monuments, statues, and plaques dispersed throughout the street celebrating famous people and events. Amongst these are also some eye-catching statues and monuments that appear out of context to locals and visitors alike. One structure is a miniature lighthouse located on George Street in New Town. At first glance, the small lighthouse would appear to be a building decoration, advertising the local business. In fact, throughout history, it is common practice to place 3-D structures outside of a home or business. For example, Gladstone Landing has a hawk mounted just outside the entrance door, advertising the Gled family name.

However, the true purpose of this lighthouse is fascinating. The miniature lighthouse is equipped with a revolving light, placed outside of the Northern Lighthouse Board since 1950. Monitoring a total of 208 lighthouses and 174 buoys, the Northern Lighthouse Board has served as marine navigational assistance since 1786. [ccxli]

Though somewhat overshadowed by his more well-known grandson, the grandson who wrote The Strange Case of Dr. Jekyll and Mr. Hyde, Robert Stevenson (1772–1850) was one of Edinburgh's most well-known civil engineers. Robert Stevenson is credited with designing many lighthouses in Scotland (1794-1833). He oversaw the construction of the lighthouse on the Isle of Little Cumbrae at the age of 19. At the age of 26, Stevenson became the superintendent of the Northern Lighthouse Board, and by 1808, he had become the sole engineer of all lighthouses under the board's authority in the region.

The Bell Rock Lighthouse. [By Percival Skelton.]

ccxlii

*Bell Rock Lighthouse*

One of his most challenging projects was the lighthouse construction at Bell Rock. Stevenson designed the lighthouse to be 100 feet, to stand against the violent surging waves of the North Sea. He applied new technology, incorporating the latest oil lighting methods to increase the illumination of the light projected from the reflectors. Despite the North Sea's stormy weather, Bell Rock's construction is acknowledged as an engineering marvel. In addition to being the nation's leading civil engineer, Robert Stevenson also paved the way for his three sons, his wife, and his grandkids to carry on his legacy of 150 Scottish lighthouse constructions. [ccxliii]

On the third weekend of September, visitors can pop in for tours and lectures on the Northern Lighthouse Board's 'Open Door Days.' Visitors should be on the lookout for the miniature lighthouse mounted on the Northern Lighthouse Board.

# Princes Street Gardens

ccxliv/ccxlv

*The Ross Fountain*

| Free access | Princes Street, Edinburgh, EH2 2HG, UK |
|---|---|

Nor Loch was once a beautiful lake near the northern side of Edinburgh Castle. Originally, Nor Loch began as a stream called East Fowl Burn, which had been dammed up in the 15th century, as ordered by King James III. In time, the blocked stream began to fill with water, creating Nor Loch. The location of the loch not only provided water for the town but also doubled as a defense against invading forces. During the 17th century, the town became heavily populated as the city expanded, and the loch became the dumping grounds for the city's sanitation runoffs. During the 17th century the town expanded, and the Loch became a hindrance, as it limited the expansion opportunities. In addition, by 1756, the pollution of Nor Loch had become an unbearable cesspool of toxic waste, and the decision to drain the loch was greatly anticipated by the city. Remember 'Auld Reekie'? Although the Loch was drained during Edinburgh's expansion, the East Fowl Burn stream remains in its original place but is underground. The unmarked location is hard to find but hidden away under a square metal plate near Ross Fountain, the stream still flows. The former Nor Loch became Princes Garden. The drained Nor Loch became a private garden with a canal running through, but the plans were modified to adapt to the mounting 1.5 tons of debris left over during the construction of New Town. The mound is located on a street that joins Old Town from New Town, cutting Princes Street Gardens into two sections down the middle. This disrupted Craig's original design. As a result, Princes Street had been changed from its original linear line to two separate gardens divided by the mound. The original plans to include the tranquil canal were eliminated and changed to accommodate the mound; the cost to remove the mound exceeded the city's budget. [ccxlvi]

With construction plans changed, the area became transformed into a posh private residence for the wealthy with private access to the two gardens. Residents were given keys to access the privately opened gardens free of charge. The only time the private gardens were opened to the public was on Christmas Day and New Year's Day. By 1876, the gardens were opened to the public every day.

Remnants of the old townhomes are hard to find, since the homes were torn down or transformed into shops. Although much of the original homes have changed, a few buildings managed to sustain the original design of the Georgian era home. The Booty Cow Pub has some elements reminiscent of 18th century homes. Located on George St, the pub has the original servants' quarters located downstairs, accessed from the street, and the families' quarters located on street level. The original townhomes designed by James Craig, have been nearly erased from the landscape along Princes Street Gardens. Growing concern about future construction in the park rallied the citizens of Edinburg to petition Parliament to pass the Order of Confirmation Act in 1991. The law banned the construction of any future buildings in the park. The people did not want the view of Edinburgh Castle to be obstructed by tall buildings. The Balmoral Hotel is the last building constructed before the law was passed. Any building built after the law passed must be subterranean or underground to protect the view of the castle.

ccxlvii

### *Floral Coo Coo Clock*

One remarkable site to see is the famed Floral Coo Coo Clock, created in 1903, on the east end of the mound. It is the oldest floral clock remaining. Each year, the floral clock must be planted in the ground. The fully functioning clock has hands, numbers, and a floral display. In 1973, an electric motor was added to ensure the clock hands would continue to move. Prior to 1973, the clock had to be manually wound each day. Throughout July to October, the floral clock is meticulously cared for by two gardeners.

The Floral Clock is just one of the amazing things to see while visiting Princes Street Gardens. There is a second clock of notes, the Balmoral clock, at the Balmoral Hotel. This clock runs 3 minutes late. This is intentional due to the hotel's proximity to the Waverley train station. The clock runs slow to allow people a few minutes to catch the train. During New Year's Eve, the clock is set to the correct time to welcome the New

Year. After New Year's Day, the clock is set three minutes forward once again.[ccxlviii] Throughout the park, there are many statues stationed along the pathways celebrating famous people in Edinburgh.

One interesting statue is a statue of a boy and a bear located in the garden. The story behind the unusual statue dates to 1942, when a local boy found a newly born baby bear laying near his mother, who had been fatally shot. With no one to care for the infant bear, the boy took the newborn cub home. After the bear grew, the boy sold the bear to soldiers in the Polish army on their way to Tehran. Wojtek, the bear, soon became very attached to the soldiers, and they had grown very fond of him. When the troop was ordered to transfer to Italy, they decided to take Wojtek with them instead of leaving him behind. Wojtek was not only the troop's mascot, but he also participated in many battles and served the troop by carrying supplies and weapons along the way.

ccxlix /ccl

*Wojtek - soldier*

222

In the beginning, feeding Wojtek was a struggle. Eventually, he was fed condensed milk from a vodka bottle and picked up some rather unpleasant habits from the soldiers, learning to drink beer and smoke. During the war, Wojtek began his military life as a private, and was later promoted to corporal, for his aid in carrying supplies for the troop. After WWII ended, Wojtex could no longer accompany the soldiers after the unit was demobilized in 1947 and spent the remainder of his life at the Edinburgh Zoo until he passed away at the age of 21. Wojtex's statue is a memorial to the Polish soldiers' efforts in fighting against the threat of fascism during WWII and celebrates the alliance between the Scots and the Polish people.

ccli /cclii /ccliii

*(left side) Dr. James Simpson (right side) Sir Walter Scott*

223

Dr. James Simpson's statue is dedicated to his contributions to the medical field. He was known for his work in inventing chloroform and anesthesia.

The most imposing monument in Princes Street Garden is Sir Walter Scott's monument, the second tallest monument (200 feet) in the world. Designer George Kemp created the 3-level monument (1844 or 1846) to express Scott's great achievements. Known for his romantic literary novels, the Waverley books, Scott revitalizes the rich history of the Highland Scots and the Jacobite Rebellion in 1745. His novels evoke a sense of nationalism among the Scottish people. Throughout the Waverley novels, Scott orchestrates a romantic revival of Scottish heritage.

Scott is given credit for succeeding in overturning the English law by 1782, that forbade Scots from wearing their clan tartans. Through a conversation with the King, Scott "convinced King George IV that he was every bit as much a genuine Jacobite Highland King as any of his predecessors." [ccliv]

Scott is also known for his discovery of the Honors of Scotland. During the time when Oliver Cromwell was Regent of England, the Honors of Scotland (royal jewels and silver scepters) were removed and hidden between 1651-1660. Upon the passing of the Acts of Union in 1707, the Honors of Scotland were sealed in a chest and hidden away once again. Many people had come to believe the Honors of Scotland were lost forever, but in 1818, Sir Walter Scott found the Honors and the silver scepter, reuniting Scotland with the royal jewels of past Scottish kings.[cclv]

> ### Honors of Scotland Found
>
> On February 4, 1818, Scott, and a team, of workmen went down into the bowels of the Castle to a storage room in which lay an old wooden box. Breaking open the box was 'neither an easy nor a speedy task' as Scott himself put it. Eventually the lid was raised and there lay the Honours, wrapped in the same linen cloths which had surrounded them for 110 years.

cclvi

Today, Sir Walter Scott's monument is a reminder of the significant impact the novelist had in reviving the Scottish identity and nationalism of the people.

# Historical Monuments
# in Edinburgh

cclvii

Adam Black (1784-1874) is known as a liberal politi-cian and a reformer during his time in Parliament when the topic of suffrage and parliament reform was highly debated. In addition, Black's publishing company is known for obtaining the copyrights to publish the En-cyclopedia Britannica and the Waverly novels in 1851.

cclviii

David Livingstone was an ordained Minister sent to South Africa. He discovered Victoria Falls. He passed in 1873 during his quest to search for the source of the Nile River. Livingstone's statue holds a Bible in his hand and wears a cloak with a haversack, a pistol, and a compass. Draped at the base is lion skin, which demonstrates the time when he successfully survived a lion mauling.

cclix

Professor Wilson is known as an influential thinker and a professor of Moral Philosophy. Wilson used the false name of Christopher North to insert his view of anti-reform, published works in Blackwood Magazine. His articles caused an uproar among people who did not share his beliefs on the issue. Allen Ramsay designed Wilson's statue holding the manuscript of John Steell with a contemplative pose.

cclx

Allen Ramsay (1685-1758) is credited for the opening of the first British circulating library along the Royal Mile. He is also remembered for reviving Scottish vernacular satirical humour poetry through his works, The *Gentle Shepherd*. The statue is composed of Carrara marble boasting the height of 10 ft. Sir John Steell was commissioned to create the statue, which has Ramsay wearing a nightcap on his head instead of a traditional wig, giving homage to him as a wig maker. The nightcap signifies the late hours he would work making wigs in his younger years.

cclxi

This statue designed by William Brodie is entitled "the Genius Architecture" The statue depicts a woman with two children who represent the Theory of Practice of Art.

cclxii

This imposing genesis boulder was given to General Sir Roland Gibbs, the Lord Provost Borthwick, on Sept 18, 1978, by the Norwegian Army. On the boulder is the inscription, "During the war years 1940-1945 the Norwegian brigade and other army units were raised and trained in Scotland where we found hospitality, friendship, and hope during dark years of exile. In grateful memory of our friends and allies of these isles. This stone was erected in the year 1978." On the backside, "This boulder was brought here from Norway where it was worn and shaped for 1,000s years by force of nature-frost, running water, rock, sand and ice-unit it obtained its present shape."

cclxiii

Robert Tait Mackenzie created the memorial during 1924-1927. The plinth holds the inscription, "The Call 1914. A Tribute from Men and Women of Scottish Blood and Sympathies in the United States of America to Scotland. A People that jeopardizes their lives unto death in the High Places of the Field" The relief on the backdrop depicts of Scottish men working miners, shepherds, gamekeepers, farmers, and fishermen, being hailed to war by the regimental pipe and drum band. A second inscription reads, "If it be life that waits, I shall live forever unconquered, if death, I shall die, at last, strong in my pride and free." Entitled, 'A Creed' poem was written at Vimy Ridge in 1916 by Lt. E. Alan Mackintosh (1883-1917) the 5th Seaforth Highlanders, 51st Highland Division.

cclxiv

This statue was designed by William Birnie Rhind and is placed in Princes Street Gardens on November 16, 1906. The statue honors a Royal Scots Dragoon Guard astride his horse. He is in full military uniform complete with the traditional bearskin hat. The French eagle insignia on the plaque was adopted after its capture by the Ensign Ewart during The Battle of

Waterloo. The plaques commemorate the losses during both the WWI and WWII wars.

cclxv

    This statue depicts Thomas Guthrie holding a bible in his arms while gazing down at a child. Designed by Frederick W. Pomeroy, the statue commemorates Guthrie's historical significance as an educator at Edinburgh University. Guthrie led the establishment of the Free St. John's church located on Castle Hill. In 1862, he became the Moderator of the Free Church Assembly. Guthrie is also known for his publication "Plea for the Ragged Schools and the City its Sin and Sorrows". On the platform is inscribed, "Thomas Guthrie D.D (Doctor of Divinity), preacher and philanthropist 1803-1873, born at Bechin, Forfarshire, and eloquent preacher of the gospel, founder of the original ragged

industrial schools, and friend of the poor and op-
pressed."

cclxvi

In December 2012, the Mortonhall Cremato-
rium Scandal brought to light the dishonest practices of
the local crematorium. A total of 250 premature babies
were cremated, but the family was never given the
ashes of their babies. The *Daily Record reported*, "The
baby ashes scandal emerged in December 2012 when it
was revealed that the council-run crematorium had buried or scattered the ashes of babies for decades without
their relatives' knowledge."cclxvii

Within the report, Mathieson revealed that the
deceased baby's bodies were placed in the cremation in
the evening and were left for the morning when adult
cremations were done. When parents asked for the
ashes of their infant, the facility informed the families
that it was common to not have any ashes from the in-
fants after the cremation process was done. The scandal brought the situation to light, and as a result instituted laws to prevent the atrocity from happening
again. The cute, bronzed statue of a baby elephant was

234

designed by Andy Scott and placed in Princes Street Gardens in 2019. The memorial was created in memory of the babies and their loved ones who suffered by the acts of the Morton hall Crematorium. The sculptor's image of an elephant was to demonstrate that what had happened will never be forgotten, just like an elephant 'never forgets.'

# Arthur's Seat

cclxviii / cclxix

Free admission

Queen's Dr. Holyrood Pk.,
Edinburgh, EH8 8HG, UK

Ancient Celtics legend describes a dragon that used to
fly around the sky, tormenting the local villages and
consuming all the livestock. It is said that the dragon
stuffed himself to death. Engorged, he lay resting upon
the highest of the seven hills and went to sleep, never
to wake again. On a clear day, the ridges of the seven
hills form the silhouette of a sleeping dragon.

Looming above the city of Edinburgh are seven
hills deriving from an old volcano. The hills now encompass Holyrood Park. Among the hills is the highest
hill, known as Arthur's Seat, reaching a height of 800

236

feet above sea level. Its name can be misleading, seemingly connected to the ancient city of Camelot; however, there is no evidence for this belief. Not much is known about the origin of its name, although the name itself can be traced to the 15th century. William Maitland suggests a theory about the origins of Arthur's Seat being derived from the Scot Gaelic word 'Ard-na-said,' translated as 'Height of Arrows.' Today, Maitland's theory is believed to be the closest view of the origins of the name.

Over time, the words began to blend, forming the pronunciation of Arthur's Seat. The 'Seat' refers to an alcove nearly halfway up the hill between the second peak and the highest peak. A moderate 2-hour hike up Arthur's Seat offers a unique opportunity for locals and visitors to view the city of Edinburgh from a panoramic view.

Arthur's Seat, while beautiful, is shrouded in mystery and myth. The story takes place in 1836, when two boys hiked Arthur's Seat to hunt for rabbits that had been known to inhabit the hills near Holyrood Palace. Along the way, the boys discovered a small cave hidden away within the rock. As they investigated the cave, they discovered three pointed slates. Sparked with curiosity, the boys removed the slab lid and found 17 miniature coffins. The miniature coffin measured 3-4 inches in length and held wooden people all dressed in different period clothing.

Excited by their discovery, the boys weren't very careful with the miniature coffins. As a result, of the 17, only 8 remained intact. Eventually, the remaining coffins were given to Robert Frazier, South Andrews Jeweler. After receiving the unique artifacts, he displayed the miniature coffins in his personal museum. In 1845, Fraizer retired, and his private collection was auctioned off. [cclxx] The coffins were sold for 4 pounds. The miniature coffins disappeared after the sale until 1901, when the set was donated to the National Museum of Scotland.

While in the museum, the coffins underwent further study, and scientists concluded the coffins were not the same age. They theorized the coffins were added over the years and buried in three levels, with the oldest layer at the bottom and the newer coffins at the top. One theory surrounding the origins of the coffins was brought forth by *The Scotsman, The Edinburgh Evening Post, and the Caledonian Mercury in 1901.* A second story later emerged in 1906 when the *Scotsman* reported about a lady living in Edinburgh, stating that "her father ('Mr. B.') had been visited at his business by a 'daft man'. On one occasion, the man had drawn on a piece of paper a picture of three small coffins, with the dates 1837, 1838, and 1840 written underneath. In the autumn of 1837, "*The Scotsman* explains, "a near relative of Mr. B died; in the following year, a cousin died; and in 1840, his own brother died. After the funeral, the deaf-mute man appeared again, walked into Mr. B's office, and 'glaring' at him and vanishing, never to return." "Is it not possible?" The article continues, "that this man was the maker of Arthur's Seat coffins, driven mad by the loss of his treasures." [cclxxi]

The miniature coffins remain one of the many bizarre stories surrounding the city of Edinburgh.

# St. Catherine's Well – Balms Well

cclxxii

St. Catherine's Balm Well
Howden Rd.LB28122

St. Catherine's Well, commonly known as Balm Well, is a small structure tucked away in a field located south of Libberton village. The ancient well has been written about throughout history by writers such as Mathew Mackaile (1664) and George Good (1893). Good wrote:

*"A very ancient chapel was dedicated to St. Catherine, which stood with its burying-ground near the modern mansion of St. Catherine's. All trace of this chapel has disappeared, but at the end of last century its ruins were still extant. It was reputed to be the most ancient place of worship in the parish, and the ground around the chapel was consecrated for burials. Hither came annually in solemn procession the nuns from the Convent of Sciennes, a foundation due to the piety of one of the St. Clairs of Rosslyn, who may possibly have also been connected with the origin of the Chapel of St. Catherine."*

-George Good (1893)

cclxxiii

Travelers from all over Europe and Scotland were cured of their illnesses after James Begg (1845) reported that the well in his parish of Libberton had therapeutic abilities.

*"At St Catherine's, there is the famous well, before alluded to, anciently called the Balm Well. Black oily substances constantly float on the surface of the water. However, many you remove they still appear to reside in this well, and it was much frequented by persons afflicted with cutaneous complaints. The nuns of the Sheens made an annual procession to it in honour of St Catharine. King James VI visited it in 1617 and ordered it to be properly enclosed and provided with a door and staircase, but it was destroyed and filled up by the soldiers of Cromwell in 1650. It has again been opened and repaired and is now in a good state of preservation."*
-James Bregg

cclxxiv/cclxxv

Both King James IV and King James VI visited the well during their lives and valued the well for its religious meaning and healing components. The Well soon gathered fame for its miracle cures. Although it is important to note that scientists have not found any supernatural healing qualities in the oily well water. Many people suffering from different ailments found that the well's oily water (8.45 soluble sulfate, chloride, alkali, and 19.66 insoluble calcareous carbonates) provided relief from their ailments of the skin, mainly eczema. The oily substance which gave the well its unique healing effects is believed to have come from a

241

fault line. Today, the original Well House has been re-placed with a newer design. The entrance is blocked to keep out visitors, but people can still walk by and see the famous Healing Well of St. Catherine near Toby Carvery.

# Muschats Cairn

cclxxvicclxxvii

It seems at every turn another memorial marks a pinnacle point in the history of Edinburgh. Some statues and memorials stand out and have an imposing stature surrounding them, while other memorials appear to be less distinguished in their impact. The Witches Well in the Castle Esplanade is one that is often overlooked under the immense size of Edinburgh Castle. Smaller memorials, like the one depicted above, are usually looked over, but their significance is equal to the grander statues and memorials throughout the city.

      The Muschats Cairn in Holyrood Park is known as the 'forgotten memorial.' At first glance, this memorial can be overlooked as a pile of rocks. There is no way to reveal the sad story behind the memorial, but this Cairn reveals the sad fate of a woman murdered by her husband.

In 1720, the town's surgeon, Nichol Muschat, committed a heinous act of murder. Muschat confessed that he brought his wife, Ailie Muschat, to Holyrood Park and murdered her. When he was interrogated about his crime, he revealed that this was not his first attempt to free himself from her. He had initially attempted to poison her, but that had failed. His second plan was to accuse her of infidelity and ruin her reputation, and this, too, had failed. Another attempt was to have his friend kill her, but this also failed. In his final act to free himself from his marriage, he lured her to the park and murdered her.

During his trial, he was asked why he murdered her. His answer was shocking to hear. He was simply bored of her. Muschat was sentenced to be hanged at Grassmarket, the execution site in Edinburgh. A traditional Scottish Cairn was erected at the original murder site near St. Anthony, as a memorial to Ailie Muschat. Over time, people added stones to Cairns, expanding the memorial's footprint. Unfortunately, no marker was erected at the site, and local guidebooks also fail to mention Ailie Muschat in the retelling of the event. According to legend, the significance of the memorial left such an impact on King George IV that he wanted to see the memorial when he would visit Holyrood Palace, so he requested the Cairns be moved to Holyrood Park in the 1800s.

Today, Ailie Muschat's Memorial can be seen on the eastern edge of Holyrood Park, left of St. Margaret's Loch. Viewers should spend some time viewing Edinburgh's most "Forgettable Memorial" in remembrance of Ailie Maschat, who was murdered by her husband Nichol Maschat because he was tired of her.

244

Her story is all but forgotten in history, and the only reminder of her is an unlabeled mound of rocks dedicated to her memory. [cclxxviii]

# Only in Scotland

There was a myth in Scotland that if a Scotsman died outside of Scotland, their soul or spirit would travel through the earth to arrive within the borders of the country. This was called taking the "Low Road." A famous song is *Loch Lomond*. Often, this song is sung on joyous occasions, but the song carries a heavier tone. The lyrics tell of a person's death, their soul transported to Scotland through the low road (the earth) while their loved one treads on the high road. The tune laments that neither will meet again on the bonnie banks of Loch Lomond.

## Loch Lomond

*By yon bonnie banks and by yon bonnie braes.*
*Where the sun shines bright on Loch Lomond*
*Where me and my true love spent many happy days*
*On the bonnie banks of Loch Lomond*
*T'was there that we parted in yon shady glen.*
*On the steep sides of Ben Lomond*
*Where in purple hue the Highlands hills we view*
*And the moon glint out in the gloaming*
*{Chorus}*
*You'll take the high road and I'll that the low road.*
*And I'll be in Scotland afore ye.*
*Where me and my true love **will never meet again**.*
*On the bonnie bonnie banks of Loch Lomond.*
*Verse 2:*
*Where wildflowers spring and the wee birdies sing*
*On the steep, steep side of Ben Lomond*
*But the broken heart it kens nae second spring.*
*Through resigned we may be while we're greetin'*
*{Repeat Chorus}*

# Window Tax 1748

cclxxix

A government, monarch, or ruling power of a country always needs capital to pay for expenses to run a civilization. How the governing body acquires funds is usually in the form of taxing the citizens within the country. Unique ways to find additional ways to gain extra revenue are always cleverly found and some can be quite bizarre, to say the least. One such method of taxation was implemented in Edinburgh, Scotland in 1748 to tax the wealthier people in town. The assumption for the tax was that richer people in the community could afford a nicer home and the homes with the most windows would indicate that the owner had a higher income. Under this theory, the government passed a law to tax homes by the number of windows each residence had, known as the window tax. The more windows one had the higher the resident would be taxed.

Well, let's just say that the people were not thrilled over being taxed based on the number of windows they had. So, in true Scottish fashion, the residents began removing the windows and filling the void with stone. Some owners decided not to remove the window but just painted the window black so that the government could not tell if there was a window or not. Since the tax was not determined by the frame of the window rather it was based upon the actual window, the people successfully found a loophole in the taxation law. Throughout Edinburgh, when looking carefully at the old buildings the windows have been blocked, and the framework of the window still exists without the glass. Although a positive loophole was discovered to get out of paying a higher tax there were negative effects of the law.

As people continued to block their windows the community began to exhibit higher cases of illness due to the lack of vitamin D, which is produced by the sun. The tax was coined Daylight Robbery or viewed as a tax on light and air. The tax was instituted upon the Scots to help England pay the war expenses in the war against France. From 1748 to 1820, this tax proved to be popular with parliament and the fee steadily increased over the years. Continual resistance eventually gained in favor for the Scots in 1851 when the tax finally came to an end and was repealed. Today, one can see the Scottish defiance against the Crown's taxation on windows by the lasting reminder of a tax that darkened Scotland.

# Edinburgh's Closes, Wynds, and Courts

## Castlehill

**South:**

- Castle Wynd
- Old Distillery (private)
- Boswell's Court (private)

**North:**

- Skinner's Close (sign only)
- Semple Close (sealed)
- Jollie's Close (sealed)

## High Street

**South:**

- Barrie's Close (connects Parliament Sq. to Fishmarket Close)
- Old Fishmarket Close (open)
- Borthwick's Close (connect Tron sq)
- Old Assembly Close
- Covenant Close (private)
- Burnet's Close (private)
- Bell's Wynd (connects to Tron sq)
- New Assembly Close
- Steven law's Close (connects to Cowgate)
- Marlin's Wynd
- Dickson's Close (sign only)

**North:**

- Byer's Close (private)
- Advocates Close (connects to Crockburn Street.)
- Roxburgh Close (upper and lower blocked)
- Writer's Close (connects to Cockburn Street.)
- Mary King's Close
- Craig's Close (access fr. Crockburn Street and connects to Market Street)

- Anchor Close (connect Cockburn Street)
- Geddes Entry (private)
- North Foulis Close (private)
- Old Stamp Office Close (private)
- Lyon's Close (private)
- Jackson's Close Connect to Cockburn Street)
- Fleshmarket Close (connect to Market Street)
- Bishop's Close (private)
- North Gray's Close (connect to Jeffrey Street)
- Morrison's Close (private)
- Bailie Fyfe's Close (dead end)
- Paisley Close (dead end)
- Chalmer's Close (private)
- Monteith Close (private)
- Trunk's Close (private)
- Baron Maule's Close (private)

## Castlehill
**South:**
- Castle Wynd
- Old Distillery (private)
- Boswell's Court (private)

**North:**
- Skinner's Close (sign only)
- Semple Close (sealed)
- Jollie's Close (sealed)

## Lawnmarket
**South:**
- Riddle's Court (dead end)
- Fisher's Close (opened)
- Brodie's Close (open to Fisher Close)
- Buchanan's Close (open to Fisher Close)

**North:**
- Mylne's Close (open)
- James Court (open)
- Lady Stair's Close (open)
- Wardrop's Close (open)

## Canongate
**South:**

- Gullans' Close (connecting to Holyrood Road)
- Gibb's Close (sign only/ serves solely as access to a shop)
- Pirrie's Close (connecting to Chessel's Court)
- Old Playhouse Close (sealed/ private dead end)
- Sugarhouse Close
- Bakehouse Close
- Wilson's Court
- Cooper's Close
- Crichton's Close
- Bull's Close (connecting to Holyrood Road)
- Reid's Close (currently no sign/ connects to Holyrood Road))
- Vallence's Entry (no sign/ private dead end)

**North:**

- Midcommon Close (sealed & private dead end)
- Bowling Green Close (leading to Gladstone's Court)
- Big Jack's Close (pedestrian access to Sibbald Walk)
- Old Tolbooth Wynd (vehicle access from Calton Road)
- Dunbar's Close (leading to a knot garden)
- Panmure Close (partly sealed over newly built extension)
- Brown's Court (dead end)
- Lochend Close (vehicular access from Calton Road)
- Gladstone's Court (private/ dead end)
- Reid's Court (the old Canongate manse)
- Campbell's Close (cranked connection to Calton Road)
- Brown's Close (dead end)
- Forsyth's Close (sealed/ private dead end)
- Galloway's Entry (dead end)
- White Horse Close (site of a coaching inn; extensively restored)

# Endnotes

i Wikimedia, "Edinburgh Castle," Accessed May 28, 2023, https://commons.wikimedia.org/wiki/File:Edinburgh_Castle_Autumn.jpg.

ii A volcanic plug is formed when the magma of the volcano hardens and essentially fills the void of the hole in which the volcano would release its lava. So, the castle is built upon the hardened magma plug of the dormant volcano.

iii For a brief timeline of the War of Independence, refer to: Scottish Historical Society, "The War of Independence," Accessed January 13, 2023, https://scottishhistorysociety.com/the-wars-of-independence/.

iv Johnson, Ben, "The Battle of Flodden," Accessed March 13, 2023, https://www.historic-uk.com/HistoryUK/Historyof-Scotland/The-Battle-of-Flodden/.

v Edinburgh Castle, "History of the Castle," Accessed January 13, 2023, https://www.edinburghcastle.scot/the-castle/history#:~:text=The%20castle%20is%20the%20most,1715%20things%20to%20poor%20planning.

vi Moczygemba, Charron. October 2023.

vii Ibid.

viii Ibid.

ix Wikipedia, "Fredrick Augustus," Accessed November 2, 2023, https://en.wikipedia.org/wiki/Prince_Frederick,_Duke_of_York_and_Albany.

x Moczygemba, Charron. October 2023.

xi Hill, Dave & Margie, "Edinburgh Castle," Accessed May 28, 2023, https://www.flickr.com/photos/the-consortium/8932217904.

xii Moczygemba, Charron. October 2023.

xiii Ibid.

xiv Ibid.

xv Ibid.

xvi Ibid.

xvii Ibid,

[xviii] All About Edinburgh, "Ensign Ewart," Accessed April 18, 2023, https://www.allaboutedinburgh.co.uk/ensign-ewart-battle-standard.

[xix] Moczygemba, Charron. October 2023.

[xx] BBC, "New drone view of William Wallace's 'hidden fort," Accessed January 31, 2023, https://www.bbc.com/news/uk-scotland-south-scotland-52536578.

[xxi] Baker, Neal, "Who was Robert the Bruce? When was he King of Scots? When did he die? And did he fight with William Wallace? Accessed January 31, 2023, https://www.thesun.co.uk/news/7069636/robert-the-bruce-king-of-scots-william-wallace-die/.

[xxii] Atlas Obscura, "William Wallace and Robert the Bruce Statutes," Accessed January 31, 2023, https://www.atlasobscura.com/places/william-wallace-and-robert-the-bruce-statues.

[xxiii] Edinburgh Experts, "Mythbusting Braveheart," Accessed January 31, 2023, https://www.edinburghexpert.com/blog/mythbusting-bravehear.

[xxiv] Moczygemba, Charron. October 2023.

[xxv] Johnson, Ben, "Edinburgh," Accessed January 13, 2023, https://www.historic-uk.com/HistoryMagazine/DestinationsUK/Edinburgh/.

[xxvi] King Edwin of Northumbria, although rumored, the city's name may have originated during 600 A.D. as "Din Eidyn or Fort of Eidyn ".

[xxvii] The Jacobite Rebellion of 1712 and 1745 gave rise to a higher ratio of the country's population moving into the town of Edinburgh.

[xxviii] Lila, "Witches' Well," Accessed May 28, 2023, https://commons.wikimedia.org/wiki/File:Witches_Well.jpg.

[xxix] Moczygemba, Charron. October 2023.

[xxx] Women often tried as witches were those who practiced medical skills, unpopular non-conformists, or women who conflicted with others in town.

[xxxi] HIS, "Witch's Well," Accessed January 9, 2023, https://memorialdrinkingfountains.word-press.com/2014/12/02/witches-well/.

[xxxii] Ibid.

[xxxiii] Worrall, Tony, "Cannonball Inn," Accessed May 28, 2023, https://www.flickr.com/photos/to-nyworrall/5872461168.

[xxxiv] Wolfblur, "Camera Obscura," Accessed May 28, 2023, https://pixabay.com/da/photos/camera-obscura-edinburgh-skotland-1591147/.

[xxxv] Chalmers, Tori, "Reasons to Visit Camera Obscura," Accessed February 28, 2023, https://theculturetrip.com/eu-rope/united-kingdom/scotland/articles/reasons-to-visit-cam-era-obscura-and-world-of-illusions-in-edinburgh/.

[xxxvi] Chalmers, Tori, "Reasons to Visit Camera Obscura," Accessed February 28, 2023, https://theculturetrip.com/eu-rope/united-kingdom/scotland/articles/reasons-to-visit-cam-era-obscura-and-world-of-illusions-in-edinburgh/.

[xxxvii] Unsplash, "Camera Obscura," Accessed May 28, 2023, https://www.istockphoto.com/search/2/image?al-lowed use=available foralluses mediatype=photography phrase=Scotland%20St.%20girls%20Jenny%20 Geddes Sort=best &page=2.

[xxxviii] Astronomical Society of Edinburgh, "A Guide to Edin-burgh's Popular Observatory," Accessed February 28, 2023, https://www.astronomyedinburgh.org/about-us/a-guide-to-edinburghs-popular-observatory/.

[xxxix] Moczygemba, Charron. October 2023.

[xl] Ibid.

[xli] Kartzsch, Ina, "Scotland Sunset at the Hub, Edinburgh Poster," Accessed January 23, 2023, https://fineartamer-ica.com/featured/scotland-sunset-at-the-hub-in-edinburgh-ina-kratzsch.html?product=poster.

[xlii] Moczygemba, Charron. October 2023.

[xliii] Planes, Trains, and Everything, "EXPLORING THE MYSTERIOUS CLOSES OF EDINBURGH'S ROYAL MILE," You Tube. (8:24) Accessed February 7, 2023, https://www.youtube.com/watch?v=4hQ MpJh 9.

xliv Close's, Wynds, and Court are listed at the end of the Scottish Brochure.

xlv Marjoribanks, Andy, "Riddle's Court," Accessed February 7, 2023, https://edinburghcabtours.com/riddles-court/.

xlvi Marjoribanks, Andy, "Riddle's Court," Accessed February 7, 2023, https://edinburghcabtours.com/riddles-court/.

xlvii Ibid.

xlviii Andraszy, "Deacon Brodie's Tavern: Edinburgh," Accessed May 28, 2023, https://commons.wiki-media.org/wiki/File:Deacon_Brodie%27s_Tavern,_Edin-burgh.jpg.

xlix Picryl, "The Strange Story of Dr. Jekyll and Mr. Hyde," Accessed May 28, 2023, https://picryl.com/media/dr-jekyll-and-mr-hyde.

l Bell, Anne, "Deacon Brodie: The Real-Life Inspiration Of Dr. Jekyll and Mr. Hyde," Accessed February 6, 2023, https://www.auldreekietours.com/2020/08/deacon-brodie-the-real-life-inspiration-for-dr-jekyll-and-mr-hyde.

li All That's Interesting," Meet William Brodie, The Man Whose Double Life Inspired Dr. Jekyll And Mr. Hyde," Accessed February 6, 2023, https://allthatsinterest-ing.com/william-brodie-real-life-jekyll-hyde.

lii Moczygemba, Charron. October 2023.

liii Moczygemba, Charron. October 2023.

liv Our Edinburgh Friends, "Statue of the Royal Mile: The 5th Duke of Buccleuch," Accessed December 11, 2023, https://ouredinburghfriends.scot/2018/06/08/statues-of-the-royal-mile-the-5th-duke-of-buccleuch/.

lv Moczygemba, Charron. October 2023.

lvi Ibid.

lvii Ibid.

lviii Ibid.

lix Ibid.

lx Traynor, Kim, "Old Tolbooth Prison," Accessed May 28, 2023, https://www.geograph.org.uk/photo/3208962.

lxi Moczygemba, Charron. October 2023.

[lxii] St. Giles is the patron saint for cripples, beggars, lepers, and mentally ill.

[lxiii] Moczygemba, Charron. October 2023.

[lxiv] Ibid.

[lxv] Traynor, Kim," Alexander III statue, West door of St. Giles, Edinburgh," Accessed May 30, 2023, https://commons.wikimedia.org/wiki/File:Alexander_III_statue,_West_door_of_St._Giles,_Edinburgh.jpg.

[lxvi] Traynor, Kim, "Statue of David I on the West Door of St. Giles High Kirk, Edinburgh," Accessed May 30, 2023, https://en.wikipedia.org/wiki/File:Statue_of_David_I_on_the_West_Door_of_St._Giles_High_Kirk,_Edinburgh.jpg.

[lxvii] Moczygemba, Charron. October 2023.

[lxviii] Ibid.

[lxix] Ibid.

[lxx] Ibid.

[lxxi] Traynor, Kim, "Angel playing bagpipes, Thistle Chapel, St. Giles," Accessed May 28, 2023, https://commons.wikimedia.org/wiki/File:Angel_playing_bagpipes,_Thistle_Chapel,_St._Giles.JPG.

[lxxii] The text on the scroll picture above is extracted from the information plaque of John Knox, located in St. Giles Cathedral.

[lxxiii] The text on the scroll picture above is extracted from the information plaque of John Knox, located in St. Giles Cathedral.

[lxxiv] Ross, David, "St. Giles Cathedral," Accessed January 14, 2023, https://www.britainexpress.com/attractions.htm?attraction=1083.

[lxxv] Ross, David, "St. Giles Cathedral," Accessed January 14, 2023, https://www.britainexpress.com/attractions.htm?attraction=1083.

[lxxvi] The text on the scroll picture above is extracted from the information plaque of Jenny Geddes, located in St. Giles Cathedral

[lxxvii] Wikipedia, "Jenny Geddes," Accessed May 28, 2023, https://en.wikipedia.org/wiki/Jenny_Geddes.

[lxxviii] It is important to note that during this period, the first record of St. Giles Church was mentioned as St. Giles Cathedral.

[lxxix] Ross, David, "St. Giles Cathedral," Accessed January 14, 2023, https://www.britainexpress.com/attractions.htm?attraction=1083.

[lxxx] Britannica, "National Covenant," Accessed January 14, 2023, https://www.britannica.com/event/National-Covenant.

[lxxxi] Ibid.

[lxxxii] The text on the scroll picture above is extracted from the information plaque of the National Covenant, located in St. Giles Cathedral.

[lxxxiii] Ibid.

[lxxxiv] Moczygemba, Charron. October 2023.

[lxxxv] Rawpixel, "Trom Weighing Scale," Accessed May 28, 2023, https://www.rawpixel.com/search?page=1&similar=6283868&sort=curated&topic_group=_topics.

[lxxxvi] Moczygemba, Charron. October 2023.

[lxxxvii] Wikipedia Commons, "Original site of the Mercat Cross, High Street," Accessed May 28, 2023, https://commons.wikimedia.org/wiki/File:Original_site_of_the_Mercat_Cross,_High_Street_-_geograph.org.uk_-_1367417.jpg.

[lxxxviii] George, Ali, "Edinburgh Mercat Cross," Accessed February 28, 2023, https://blog.historicenvironment.scot/2022/09/edinburghs-mercat-cross/.

[lxxxix] Internet Archival Images, "Old Tolbooth Prison," Accessed May 28, 2023, https://www.flickr.com/photos/internetarchivebookimages/14754945896/in/photostream/.

[xc] McLean, David, "Lost Edinburgh: Old Tolbooth Prison," Accessed February 21, 2023, https://www.edinburghnews.scotsman.com/arts-and-culture/lost-edinburgh-old-tolbooth-prison-1554328.

[xci] McLean, David, "Lost Edinburgh: Old Tolbooth Prison," Accessed February 21, 2023, https://www.edinburghnews.scotsman.com/arts-and-culture/lost-edinburgh-old-tolbooth-prison-1554328.

[xcii] Moczygemba, Charron. October 2023.

[xciii] Ibid

[xciv] Chalmers, Tori, "The Story Behind Edinburgh's Heart of Midlothian," Accessed February 7, 2023, https://theculturetrip.com/europe/united-kingdom/scotland/articles/the-story-behind-edinburghs-heart-of-midlothian/.

[xcv] Moczygemba, Charron. October 2023.

[xcvi] Atlas Obscura, "David Hume's Statue," Accessed February 15, 2023, https://www.atlasobscura.com/places/david-humes-statue.

[xcvii] Miller, Noreen, "David Himes and Causation," Accessed February 28, 2023, https://slideplayer.com/slide/13407323/.

[xcviii] Kamiya, Anne, "David Hume's Theory of Causation," Accessed February 28, 2023, https://study.com/learn/lesson/david-humes-theory-causation-metaphysics-ideas-examples.html#:~:text=Hume%20saw%20causation%20as%20a,Hume%20was%20skeptical%20of%20causality.

[xcix] Moczygemba, Charron. October 2023.

[c] Meskens, Ad, "Edinburgh Grassmarket Bow Well 02," Accessed May 29, 2023, 2013. https://commons.wikimedia.org/wiki/File:Edinburgh_Grassmarket_Bow_Well_02.JPG.

[ci] In 1867, the Improvement Act was brought to Parliament by William Chambers. The law was established to improve the poor conditions within the town. Part of the population growth in town was a direct result of the potato famine sweeping throughout the country. Irish and Highland Scots seeking to find a way to earn an income and to provide for their families prompted rural farmers into the city, primarily Edinburgh. Edinburgh was also going through a transition as wealthier patrons were moving out of the old town and moving into the new town in Edinburgh. Resulting in many older buildings being abandoned. The dilapidated old building soon had rural out-of-towners quickly filling the homes. The once-large homes in the old town were quickly subdivided into smaller rooms to accommodate large families. Multiple families now occupy very small rooms within a home.

The increased population, combined with tight living conditions and poor sanitation, soon became the perfect storm in which disease and illness would soon run amuck throughout the city of Edinburgh. The Improvement Act was designed to tackle the dangerous conditions faced by the people in the city. Within the law, old buildings on the east side would be torn down, and roads would be widened to allow new buildings to be constructed to house families.

The passing of the 1867 law succeeded in tackling the dangers facing the city of Edinburgh and improving the sanitation conditions plaguing the community.

[cii] Traynor, Kim, "The Edinburgh Grassmarket by W L Leitch c.1854," Accessed May 29, 2023, https://commons.wikimedia.org/wiki/File:The_Edinburgh_Grassmarket,_c.1854.jpg.

[ciii] On February 28, 1628, a group of Scottish Presbyterians gathered at Greyfriars Kirk to sign the National Covenant. Within the Covenant, the document states, "Jesus Christ was the head of their church and not the King." The Covenanters feared the idea of the Crown having authority over religion and were increasingly concerned that the church would once again be placed under the dominion of the Papal. The signing of the National Covenant prompted a Civil War (August 22, 1642- September 3, 1651) pitting English King Charles I and the Royalists against the Scottish Covenanters, who created an alliance with Oliver Cromwell. When King Charles I was executed, the Covenanters backed King Charles II as their new king because he had promised the Covenanters religious tolerance, but he later reneged on his promise, declaring Presbyterianism illegal. King Charles II then sought to restore the Papacy.

Oliver Cromwell was furious over the Scots backing King Charles II and decided to break his alliance with the Scots and invade the country. Fearing being beheaded, King Charles II went into exile until Cromwell had died in 1658. The King reasserted his efforts to restore the Papacy. During the English Civil Wars, the covenanters were hunted, tortured, and executed by the Crown. This dark period was known as the Killing Time, costing the lives of 18,000 Christians who stood firmly in their faith. Secret open-aired meetings called Conventicles were held to continue to preach the Presbyterian message to the faithful followers. Further persecution was leveled against the believers as named were written down for those not attending Episcopalian services. The names were given to the Royalists who sought retribution against the non-attenders through forms of execution, arrest, or exile to America. Subsequent battles were fought against the Covenanters and the Crown: 1666 Rullion Green, 1679 Drumclog and Bothwell Brig. During the Battle of Bothwell Brig 1,400 Covenanters had managed to survive, to be caught and imprisoned in Greyfriars Kirk. While imprisoned he died of starvation and exposure to the elements.

Find My Past, "Scottish Covenanters 1679-1688," Accessed January 24, 2023, https://www.findmypast.com/articles/world-records/full-list-of-united-kingdom-records/newspapers-directories-and-social-history/scottish-covenanters-1679-1688#:~:text=Relief%20for%20the%20Scottish%20Presbyterians,not%20compromise%20their%20beliefs%20suffered.
[civ] David, "Covenanters Memorial, Grassmarket, Edinburgh, Scotland," Accessed May 28, 2023, https://www.flickr.com/photos/brokentaco/51037606472.
[cv] Moczygemba, Charron. October 2023.
[cvi] Tilburg, Kees, "Equestrian Statues," Accessed January 31, 2023, https://equestrianstatue.org/charles-ii/.
[cvii] Parliamentary Square, "Statutes in and Around the Square," Accessed January 31, 2023, https://parliamentsquareedinburgh.net/statues-in-and-around-the-square/.
[cviii] Tilburg, Kees, "Equestrian Statues," Accessed January 31, 2023, https://equestrianstatue.org/charles-ii/.
[cix] R. Vanessa, "Top 10 Unbelievable Facts about the Royal Mile, Accessed January 10, 2023, https://www.discoverwalks.com/blog/edinburgh/top-10-unbelievable-facts-about-the-royal-mile/.
[cx] Atlas Obscura, "Charles II Statue," Accessed January 31, 2023, https://www.atlasobscura.com/places/charles-ii-statue#:~:text=This%20life%2Dsized%20state%20of,meant%20to%20symbolize%20Imperial%20authority.
[cxi] Moczygemba, Charron. October 2023.

[cxii] Scottish Fire and Rescue Service, "Anniversary of the death of James Braidwood," Accessed March 1, 2023, https://www.firescotland.gov.uk/news/2020/june/anniversary-of-death-of-james-braidwood/.

[cxiii] Clan Broonford, "The Story of the Great Fire of Edinburgh," You Tube (15:58). Accessed March 2, 2023, https://www.google.com/search?q=you+tube+Clan+Broonford+James+Braidwood+Statue&rlz=1C1CHBF_enUS881US882&oq=you+tube+Clan+Broonford+James+Braidwood+Statue&aqs=chrome..69i57j33i10i160.13927j0j15&sourceid=chrome&ie=UTF-8#up-state=iv&v=cid:5fb1a443,vid:bkxAM5-phKI.

[cxiv] Moczygemba, Charron. October 2023.

[cxv] Laissez-faire - theory of value, price, supply, demand, and distribution without government intervention.

[cxvi] Robinhood Learn, "What is Adam Smith?" Accessed February 15, 2023, https://learn.robinhood.com/articles/1EAManQDjRJ20KWcLpOOHx/what-is-adam-smiths-economic-theory/.

[cxvii] Moczygemba, Charron. October 2023.

[cxviii] Ibid

[cxix] Trip.com, "Memorial Duke of Buccleuch," Accessed February 21, 2023, https://www.trip.com/travel-guide/attraction/edinburgh/memorial-duke-of-buccleuch-32849493/.

[cxx] Tiger Tom & Wild Will, "The Real Mary King's Close-Edinburgh- Surprise Holiday to Scotland," You Tube (Screen Shot) (4:36) Accessed May 28, 2023,https://www.youtube.com/watch?v=9jgJJ9CoWxs.

[cxxi] Atlas Obscura, "Mary King's Close," Accessed February 8, 2023, https://www.atlasobscura.com/places/mary-kings-close.

[cxxii] Atlas Obscura, "Mary King's Close," Accessed February 8, 2023, https://www.atlasobscura.com/places/mary-kings-close.

cxxiii Blakemore, Erin, "Why did the Plague Doctor Wear Those Strange Beaked Masks?, "Accessed February 8, 2023, https://i.natgeofe.com/n/d2ed0170-7dc3-4ff9-bd04-83e72070dd0b/plague-doctors-reference-01_3x2.jpg.

cxxiv Rennie, Daniel, "Inside The Terrifying But Necessary Job of A Medieval Plague Doctor," Accessed November 18, 2023, https://allthatsinteresting.com/plague-doctor.

cxxv Atlas Obscura, "Mary King's Close," Accessed February 8, 2023, https://www.atlasobscura.com/places/mary-kings-close.

cxxvi Bagtown Clans, "History and Rediscovery of Edinburgh's Vaults," You Tube. March 2023. Accessed May 29, 2023, https://www.youtube.com/watch?v=8RN0jcexr3w.

cxxvii Palmer, Claire, "Edinburgh's South Bridge and Vault," Accessed April 17, 2023, https://www.historic-uk.com/HistoryMagazine/DestinationsUK/Edinburgh-Vaults/.

cxxviii Ibid.

cxxix Moczygemba, Charron. October 2023.

cxxx The city of Thessaly, Greece, was well recognized for breeding the finest quality of horses in the region.

cxxxi Napa Valley, "The Story of Bucephalus," Accessed February 15, 2023, chrome-extension://efaidnbmnnnibp-cajpcglclefindmkaj/https://www.blackstallionwinery.com/assets/client/File/The%20Story%20of%20Bucephalus_poster.pdf.

cxxxii Moczygemba, Charron. October 2023.

cxxxiii Ibid.

cxxxiv Rawpixel, "Tron Weighing Scale," Accessed May 28, 2023, https://www.rawpixel.com/search?page=1_similar=6283868&sort=curated&topic_group=_topics.

cxxxv Ibid.

cxxxvi SHBT, "The Tron," Accessed May 28, 2023, www.shbt.org.uk.

cxxxvii Wikipedia, "Elizabeth Dundas," Accessed May 28, 2023, https://en.wikipedia.org/wiki/Elizabeth_Dundas.

cxxxviii Edinburgh World Heritage, "Writer's Museum, Lady Stair's House," Accessed April 17, 2023, https://ewh.org.uk/iconic-buildings-and-monuments/lady-stairs-house/.

cxxxix Moczygemba, Charron. October 2023.

cxl Ibid.

cxli Traynor, Kim, "Gladstone's Land," Accessed May 28, 2023, https://commons.wikimedia.org/wiki/File:Entrance_sign,_Gladstone%27s_Land,_Lawnmarket,_Edinburgh.JPG.

cxlii A covered passageway with arches on either side.

cxliii Britain Express, "Gladstone's Land, Royal Mile, Edinburgh," Accessed February 28, 2023, https://www.britain-express.com/scotland/Lothian/properties/gladstones-land.htm.

cxliv Britain Express, "Gladstone's Land, Royal Mile, Edinburgh," Accessed February 28, 2023, https://www.britain-express.com/scotland/Lothian/properties/gladstones-land.htm.

cxlv Wikipedia, "Gladstones Land," Accessed May 28, 2023, https://en.wikipedia.org/wiki/Gladstone%27s_Land.

cxlvi Moczygemba, Charron. October 2023.

cxlvii Clan Broonford, "Incredible Story of Paisley Close - Edinburgh," You Tube (15:05) 2021 Accessed March 2023, https://www.youtube.com/watch?v=bqOSJ2__Akw.

cxlviii Moczygemba, Charron. October 2023.

cxlix Ibid.

cl Britain Express, "John Knox House Royal Mile Edinburgh," Accessed January 13, 2023, https://www.britainexpress.com/scotland/Lothian/properties/John-Knox-House.htm.

cli Unsplash, "John Knox," Accessed May 28, 2023, https://www.istockphoto.com/search/2/image?alloweduse=availableforalluses&mediatype=photography&phrase=edinburgh%20scotland%20statues&sort=best&page=2.

[clii] Moczygemba, Charron. October 2023.

[cliii] R. Vanessa, "Top 10 Unbelievable Facts about the Royal Mile," Accessed January 10, 2023, https://www.discoverwalks.com/blog/edinburgh/top-10-unbelievable-facts-about-the-royal-mile/.

[cliv] History of Scotland, "Three Curious Facts You Probably Didn't Know About St Giles Cathedral in Edinburgh," Accessed January 10, 2023, https://www.historyscotland.com/history/three-curious-facts-you-probably-didnt-know-about-st-giles-cathedral/.

[clv] Moczygemba, Charron. October 2023.

[clvi] Saverio della Gatta, "Midwife with Baby on the way to Church for Christening," Accessed May 28, 2023, https://www.lookandlearn.com/history-images/YCH007144-001/Water-color-A-midwife-with-a-baby-on-the-way-to-church-for-christening.

[clvii] Moczygemba, Charron. October 2023.

[clviii] Atlas Obscura, "The Flodden Wall," Accessed February 21, 2023, https://www.atlasobscura.com/places/the-flodden-wall-edinburgh-scotland#:~:text=The%20Flodden%20Wall%20was%20completed,upon%20the%20ancient%20Scottish%20city.

[clix] Moczygemba, Charron. October 2023.

[clx] Echoes of the Past, "World's End Close in Edinburgh, Scotland," Accessed January 10, 2023, https://blosslynspage.wordpress.com/2014/01/21/worlds-end-close-in-edinburgh-scotland/.

[clxi] Moczygemba, Charron. October 2023.

[clxii] Zabowski, Robin, "Tardis Sighting in the Wild," Accessed May 28, 2023, https://www.flickr.com/photos/firepile/6107419845/.

[clxiii] Stewart, Robert, "The First UK Police Signal Box," Accessed January 23, 2023, https://british-police-history.uk/f/glasgow-city-signal-box.

[clxiv] Wikipedia, "Police Box," Accessed May 29, 2023, https://en.wikipedia.org/wiki/Police_box.

[clxv] Moczygemba, Charron. October 2023.

clxvi Henniker, Dave, "Edinburgh Police Boxes," Accessed January 23, 2023, https://theedinburghreporter.co.uk/living-in-edinburgh/edinburgh-police-boxes/.

clxvii Moczygemba, Charron. October 2023.

clxviii A laird - an owner of a large Scottish estate, ranking below an English Baron but above an English gentleman.

clxix Travel Scotland, "The Great Disruption of 1843," Accessed November 7, 2023, https://www.scotland.org.uk/history/disruption.

clxx Curious Edinburgh, "Summer House Moray House," Accessed January 22, 2024, http://curiousedinburgh.org/2018/01/29/summer-house-moray-house/.

clxxi University of Edinburgh, "Paterson's Land," Accessed January 22, 2024, https://www.ed.ac.uk/education/about-us/maps-estates-history/estates/patersons-land#:~:text=Moray%20House%20itself%2C%20with%20the%20smaller%20building%20in,the%20Act%20of%20Union%20between%20Scotland%20and%20England.

clxxii Moczygemba, Charron. October 2023.

clxxiii Undiscovered Scotland, "Canongate Kirk," Accessed November 18, 2023, https://www.undiscoveredscotland.co.uk/edinburgh/canongatekirk/index.html.

clxxiv Moczygemba, Charron. October 2023.

clxxv University of Edinburgh, "Canongate," Accessed November 16, 2023, https://www.ed.ac.uk/education/about-us/maps-estates-history/estates/the-canongate.

clxxvi Wandering Crystal, "Dark History at the Tolbooth," Accessed November 16, 2023, https://www.wanderingcrystal.com/tolbooth-tavern-edinburgh/.

clxxvii Wikipedia, "People's Museum," Accessed May 29, 2023, https://en.wikipedia.org/wiki/The_People%27s_Story_Museum.

clxxviii Museums & Galleries Edinburgh, 'The People's Story Museum," Accessed May 22, 2023, https://www.edinburghmuseums.org.uk/venue/peoples-story-museum.

clxxix Moczygemba, Charron, October 2023.

[clxxx] Wikipedia, "Queensbury House," Accessed May 29, 2023, https://en.wikipedia.org/wiki/Queensberry_House.

[clxxxi] Acts of Union signed on January 16, 1707, was the ratification of the Treaty of Union signed on May 1, 1707

[clxxxii] Welsh, Kaite, "Edinburgh's Earl's Son who ate a servant and became the 'Canongate Cannibal," Accessed April 18, 2023, https://www.edinburghlive.co.uk/news/edinburgh-news/edinburgh-earls-son-who-ate-20896328?int_source=amp_continue_reading&int_medium=amp&int_campaign=continue_reading_button#amp-readmore-target.

[clxxxiii] Ibid.

[clxxxiv] Parks, Anthony, "The Scottish Parliament," Accessed May 29, 2023, https://www.geograph.org.uk/photo/2366621.

[clxxxv] Morris, Dave, "Scottish Parliament Bike Rack," Accessed May 29, 2023, https://commons.wikimedia.org/wiki/File:Scottish_Parliament_bike_racks.jpg.

[clxxxvi] Moczygemba, Charron. October 2023.

[clxxxvii] Clan Broonford, "Three Things to Look for Along the Royal Mile," YouTube (15:12) Accessed January 24, 2023, https://www.youtube.com/watch?v=XlANCq9iyvQ.

[clxxxviii] Galloway, Claire, "The Fascinating Tale Behind Edinburgh's Unusual Sanctuary Stones," Accessed January 19, 2023, https://www.edinburghlive.co.uk/news/edinburgh-news/fascinating-tale-behind-edinburghs-sanctuary-15841161.

[clxxxix] Wikipedia, "Holyrood Palace," Accessed May 29, 2023, https://en.wikipedia.org/wiki/Holyrood_Palace.

[cxc] Clan Broonford, "A Brief History of Holyrood Palace," YouTube (19:46), Accessed March 2, 2023, https://www.youtube.com/watch?v=WFo1dzIUQjQ.

[cxci] Ridgway, Claire, "9 March 1566 – Murder of David Rizzio," Accessed March 2, 2023, https://www.tudorsociety.com/9-march-1566-murder-david-rizzio/.

[cxcii] Ibid.

[cxciii] For additional information about the turbulent life of Mary Queen of Scots; I recommend reading:

268

Fraser, Antonia. 2001. *Mary, Queen of Scots*. N.p.: Random House Publishing Group.

cxciv Burns, Margaret, "Memorial Fountain to Helen Acquroff at the Meadows, Edinburgh," Accessed May 29, 2023, https://commons.wikimedia.org/wiki/File:Memorial_Fountain_to_Helen_Acquroff_at_the_Meadows,_Edinburgh.JPG.

cxcv Hutchins. Johnathan, "Edinburgh's Bronze Statue of Bum the Dog," Accessed May 29, 2023, https://www.geograph.org.uk/photo/4315848.

cxcvi Parnell, Tom, "Balfour & Stewart," Accessed May 29, 2023, https://www.flickr.com/photos/itmpa/4431493941.

cxcvii Traynor, Kim, "Grave of the Great Lafayette, Piershill Cemetery," Accessed May 29, 2023, https://www.geograph.org.uk/photo/2272817.

cxcviii Gnomics, "Dr. Elsie Inglis," Accessed May 29, 2023, https://live.staticflickr.com/2848/11821258194_5245d7f9eb_b.jpg.

cxcix Haklai, Yair, "Statue of Sir Walter Scott by Sir John Robert Steell on the Scott Monument in Princes Street Gardens, Edinburgh," Accessed May 29, 2023, https://commons.wikimedia.org/wiki/File:Statue_of_Sir_Walter_Scott_by_Sir_John_Robert_Steell_on_the_Scott_Monument_in_Princes_Street_Gardens,_Edinburgh.jpg.

cc Moczygemba, Charron. October 2023

cci Ibid.

ccii Ibid.

cciii Unsplash, "Greyfriars Bobby," Accessed May 28, 2023, https://www.istockphoto.com/search/2/image?alloweduse=availableforalluses&mediatype=photography&phrase=Edinburgh%20Princes%20Street%20Gardens%20bear%20&sort=best.

cciv Murphy, Sean, "The Story Behind Greyfriars Bobby: Scotland's Most Famous Dog," Accessed January 13, 2023, https://www.dailyrecord.co.uk/scotland-now/story-behind-greyfriars-bobby-scotlands-22465887.

ccv Ibid.

269

[ccvi] Ibid.

[ccvii] Murphy, Sean, "The Story Behind Greyfriars Bobby: Scotland's Most Famous Dog," Accessed January 13, 2023, https://www.dailyrecord.co.uk/scotland-now/story-behind-greyfriars-bobby-scotlands-22465887.

[ccviii] Meskens, Ad, "Princes Street Duke of Wellington 03,"Accessed May 29, 2023, https://commons.wiki-media.org/wiki/File:Princes_Street_Duke_of_Welling-ton_03.JPG.

[ccix] National Army Museum, "Wellington: The Iron Duke," Accessed February 28, 2023,ttps://www.nam.ac.uk/ex-plore/old-nosey-duke-wellington#:~:text=A%20 lead-ing%20po litical%20and%20 military,studied%20in%20 military%20 academies%20today.

[ccx] Ibid.

[ccxi] Meskens, Ad, "Edinburgh from Calton Hill with Dugald Stewart Monument 3," Accessed May 29, 2023, https://commons.wikimedia.org/wiki/File:Edin-burgh_from_Calton_Hill_with_Dugald_Stewart_Monu-ment_3.JPG.

[ccxii] Clan Broonford, "Live Walk from Calton Hill to the New Town Edinburgh," YouTube (40:12) Accessed March 19, 2023, https://www.youtube.com/watch?v=0HTaNDsCJjl.

[ccxiii] William, "Edinburgh's Disgrace," Accessed May 29, 2023, https://www.geograph.org.uk/photo/1974130.

[ccxiv] Clan Broonford, "Live Walk from Calton Hill to the New Town Edinburgh," YouTube (40:12) Accessed March 19, 2023, https://www.youtube.com/watch?v=0HTaNDsCJjl.

[ccxv] Unsplash, "Nelson Tower, "Accessed May 28, 2023, https://www.istockphoto.com/search/2/image?al-loweduse=availableforalluses&mediatype=photog-raphy&page=3&phrase=edinburgh%20scotland%20wil-liam%20wallace%20edinburgh%20castle&sort=best.

[ccxvi] Chadwick, N., "City Observatory," Accessed May 29, 2023, https://www.geograph.org.uk/photo/2393351.

[ccxvii] Edinburgh World Heritage, "Nelson's Monument," Accessed March 19, 2023, https://ewh.org.uk/iconic-buildings-and-monuments/nelson-monument/.
[ccxviii] Ibid.
[ccxix] Moczygemba, Charron. October 2023.
[ccxx] Edinburgh World Heritage, "City Observatory," Accessed March 19, 2023, https://ewh.org.uk/project/city-observatory/.
[ccxxi] Ibid.
[ccxxii] Deagh, Dun, "Memorial to Scottish-American Soldiers of the American Civil War, Calton Hill Cemetery, Edinburgh," Accessed May 29, 2023, https://commons.wikimedia.org/wiki/File:Memorial_to_Scottish-American_Soldiers_of_the_American_Civil_War,_Calton_Hill_Cemetery,_Edinburgh_%286346003651%29.jpg.
[ccxxiii] Clan Broonford, "5 Random Edinburgh stories | Edinburgh History," You Tube. 2019. (17:58) Accessed January 18, 2023, https://www.youtube.com/watch?v=8uIWG-TuRiVU.
[ccxxiv] Moczygemba, Charron, October 2023.
[ccxxv] Atlas Obscura, "Center of Edinburgh Bollard," Accessed January 19, 2023, https://www.atlasobscura.com/places/center-of-edinburgh-bollard.
[ccxxvi] Shadowgate, "Edinburgh Dungeons," Accessed May 29, 2023, https://commons.wikimedia.org/wiki/File:Edinburgh_Dungeon_01_%28223052043%29.jpg.

[ccxxvii] Taxi & Guide, "Exploration of the Edinburgh Dungeons," Accessed April 17, 2023, https://taxiandguide.com/excursions/exploration-of-the-edinburgh-dungeon-490.
[ccxxviii] Lambda, "Royal Botanical Garden Edinburgh," Accessed May 29, 2023, https://www.flickr.com/photos/lambda_x/3608451746.
[ccxxix] Maclean, David, "Lost Edinburgh Physics Garden," Accessed May 22, 2023, https://www.scotsman.com/arts-and-culture/lost-edinburgh-the-physic-garden-1530206.

ccxxx Moczygemba, Charron. October 2023.

ccxxxi Clan Broonford, "A Walk Along Cowgate," You tube. (17:28), Accessed May 29, 2023, https://www.youtube.com/watch?v=gYNTLJDV6uM.

ccxxxii Dixon, David, "St Cuthbert's Burial Ground Watchtower," Accessed May 29, 2023, https://commons.wikimedia.org/wiki/Category:Watch_tower,_St_Cuthbert%27s_Churchyard,_Edinburgh#/media/File:St_Cuthbert's_Burial_Ground_Watchtower_-_geograph.org.uk_-_1897207.jpg.

ccxxxiii Clan Broonford, "3 unique things to do in Edinburgh," YouTube (17:02) Accessed May 20, 2023, https://www.youtube.com/watch?v=e6lVi9_FiT4.

ccxxxiv Forever Edinburgh, "Tales from beyond the Grave," Accessed January 23, 2023, https://edinburgh.org/blog/tales-from-beyond-the-grave/.

ccxxxv The wealthier people in the city would have tombs built to protect their loved ones from graverobbers.

ccxxxvi Chadwick, N, "Georgian House," Accessed May 29, 2023, https://www.geograph.org.uk/photo/2291901.

ccxxxvii Urban Network, "The city as an identity claim: the case of Edinburgh's New Town," Accessed February 1, 2024, https://urban-networks.blogspot.com/2015/06/la-ciudad-como-reivindicacion.html.

ccxxxviii Hidden Scotland, "The History of New Town," Accessed May 27, 2023, https://hiddenscotland.co/the-history-of-the-new-town/#:~:text=The%20birth%20of%20the%20New%20Town&text=The%20winning%20design%20for%20Edinburgh's,those%20who%20had%20already%20left.

ccxxxix Chinoiserie was a European interpretation of ornate Chinese design during the 17th and 18th century. The porcelain pottery, western style of furniture captivated the idea of elegance.

ccxl Moczygemba, Charron. October 2023.

ccxli Erskine, Rosalina. "There's a hidden lighthouse in the centre of Edinburgh - have you spotted it?" Edinburgh News. Feb. 24, 2020. https://www.edinburghnews.scotsman.com/node/1888832 May 17, 2023.

ccxlii Skeleton, Percival, The Bell Rock Lighthouse," Accessed February 1, 2024, https://minorvictorianwriters.org.uk/smiles/images/sr/349.jpg.

ccxliii Archer Phoenix, "5 Things You Might Not Know About Robert Stevenson, "Accessed May 17, 2023, https://blog.engineshed.scot/2020/08/06/5-things-about-robert-stevenson/.

ccxliv Solonia, Julia, "Princes Street Gardens," Accessed May 27, 2023, https://unsplash.com/s/photos/Edinburgh-Castle.

ccxlv This fountain is an example of 19th century French cast-iron work, crafted by the foundry of Antoine Durenne. Jean-Baptise Jules Klagmann sculpted the figures on the fountain. Located at the center of the fountain is a mermaid figure posed on scallop-shell basins with lion heads. The four figures illustrate science, arts, poetry, and industry with a woman holding cornucopia. Daniel Ross was commissioned to design the fountain for the Great Exhibition of 1862 in London and later gave the fountain to the city of Edinburgh. Another copy of the same fountain, though smaller in stature, is in Brazil. Outdoor Edinburgh, "Monuments in Prince Street Gardens," Accessed March 25, 2023, https://www.edinburghoutdoors.org.uk/monuments/monuments-princes-street-gardens.

ccxlvi Clan Broonford, "6 Lesser- known Things about Princes Street," YouTube (14:40) Accessed March 25, 2023, https://www.youtube.com/watch?v=y_j5LRiO_T4.

ccxlvii Unsplash, "Flora Coo Coo Clock," Accessed May 28, 2023, https://www.istockphoto.com/search/2/image?alloweduse=availableforalluses&mediatype=photography&phrase=Edinburgh%20Princes%20Street%20Gardens%20&sort=best.

ccxlviii Clan Broonford, "6 Lesser-known Things about Princes Street," YouTube (14:40) Accessed March 25, 2023, https://www.youtube.com/watch?v=y_j5LRiO_T4.

ccxlix Richardson, M J., "Wojtek in Princes Street Gardens," Accessed May 29, 2023, https://www.geo-graph.org.uk/photo/4731932.

ccl The Unofficial Guide to Edinburgh, "A Guide to Princes Street Garden in Edinburgh," Accessed January 9, 2023, https://everythingedinburgh.com/princes-street-gardens/.

ccli Richardson, M J., "Wojtek in Princes Street Gardens," Accessed May 29, 2023, https://www.geo-graph.org.uk/photo/4731932.

cclii Muhammod Shuikr, Osama, "Statue of Sir James Young Simpson, by William Brodie, 1877 CE," Accessed May 29, 2023, https://commons.wiki-media.org/wiki/File:1._Statue_of_Sir_James_Young_Simp-son,_by_William_Brodie,_1877_CE._Princes_Street,_Ed-inburgh.jpg.

ccliii Traynor, Kim, "Scott Museum, Princes Street Gardens," Accessed May 28, 2023, https://www.geo-graph.org.uk/photo/3151320.

ccliv Undiscovered Scotland, "King George IV," Accessed February 8, 2023, https://www.undiscoveredscot-land.co.uk/usbiography/monarchs/georgeiv.html.

cclv Edinburgh Castle, "Honours of Scotland," Accessed February 8, 2023, https://www.edinburghcastle.scot/see-and-do/highlights/honours-of-scot-land#:~:text=They%20where%20re-move%20from%20the,with%20a%20mysterious%20sil-ver%20wand.

cclvi The National, "How Walter Scott returned the 'Honours of Scotland' to the country," Accessed January 31, 2024, https://www.thenational.scot/news/15644419.how-walter-scott-returned-the-honours-of-scotland-to-the-country/.

cclvii Stefan Schäfer, Lich, "Adam Black Statue, Edinburgh," Accesses May 29, 2023, https://en.m.wikipe-dia.org/wiki/File:Adam_Black_Statue_Edinburgh.jpg.

cclviii Traynor, Kim, "David Livingston," Accessed May 29, 2023, https://commons.wikimedia.org/wiki/File:David_Livingstone_statue,_Princes_Street_Gardens,_Edinburgh.jpg.

cclix Traynor, Kim, "John Wilson aka 'Christopher North' statue, Princes Street Gardens," Accessed May 29, 2023, 2011,https://commons.wikimedia.org/wiki/File:John_Wilson_aka_%27Christopher_North%27_statue,_Princes_Street_Gardens.jpg.

cclx Unsplash, "Allen Ramsey," Accessed May 28, 2023, https://www.istockphoto.com/search/2/image?alloweduse=availableforalluses&mediatype=photography&phrase=edinburgh%20Adam%20Smith%20statue&sort=best.

cclxi Traynor, Kim, "Genius of Architecture statue, Princes Street Gardens," Accessed May 29, 2023, https://www.geograph.org.uk/photo/1949255.

cclxii Geograph, "The Norwegian Brigade memorial stone," Accessed November 8. 2023, https://www.geograph.org.uk/photo/2073605.

cclxiii Meskens, Ad, "Scottish American War Memorial," Accessed May 29, 2023, https://commons.wikimedia.org/wiki/File:Edinburgh_princes_Street_Gardens_The_Call_1914_04.JPG.

cclxiv Wikimedia, "Royal Scots Grey Memorial, Princes Street Gardens," Accessed February 26, 2024, https://commons.wikimedia.org/wiki/Category:Royal_Scots_Greys_Memorial,_Princes_Street_Gardens.

cclxv Traynor, Kim, "Dr Guthrie statue, Princes Street Gardens," Accessed May 29, 2023, https://www.geograph.org.uk/photo/1949254.

cclxvi Klienzack, "Mortonhall 2," Accessed May 29, 2023, https://commons.wikimedia.org/wiki/File:Wpsg_mortonhall2.jp.

[cclxvii] Mathieson, Jack, "Baby ashes scandal: Mortonhall Crematorium refused to tell parents about their babies' remains, claiming it would be 'too distressing," Accessed April 30, 2023, https://www.dailyrecord.co.uk/news/scottish-news/baby-ashes-scandal-mortonhall-crematorium-3477533

[cclxviii] Unsplash, "Arthurs Seat," Accessed May 27, 2023, https://www.istockphoto.com/photo/edinburgh-and-green-hills-in-summer-gm159128381-22667916?phrase=edinburgh+arthurs+seat.

[cclxix] National Museum of Scotland, "The Mystery of the Miniature Coffins," Accessed January 19, 2023, https://www.nms.ac.uk/explore-our-collections/stories/scottish-history-and-archaeology/mystery-of-the-miniature-coffins/.

[cclxx] Dash, Mike, "Edinburgh's Mysterious Miniature Coffins," Accessed April 15, 2023, 2013, https://www.smithsonianmag.com/history/edinburghs-mysterious-miniature-coffins-22371426/.

[cclxxi] National Museum of Scotland, "The Mystery of the Miniature Coffins," Accessed January 19, 2023, https://www.nms.ac.uk/explore-our-collections/stories/scottish-history-and-archaeology/mystery-of-the-miniature-coffins/.

[cclxxii] Moczygemba, Charron. October 2-23.

[cclxxiii] Good, George, *Liberton in Ancient and Modern Times*, Andrew Elliot: Edinburgh, 1893.

[cclxxiv] Begg, James, *"Parish of Liberton,"* in *New Statistical Account of Scotland, volume 1: Edinburgh,* William Blackwood: Edinburgh, 1845.

[cclxxv] The Northern Antiquarian, "St. Catherine's Well," Accessed November 9, 2023, https://www.thenorthernantiquarian.org/2017/06/18/st-catherines-well-liberton/.

[cclxxvii] Moczygemba, Charron, November 16, 2023.

[cclxxviii] Atlas Obscura, "Maschat Cairn," Accessed November 9, 2023, https://www.atlasobscura.com/places/muschats-cairn.

cclxxix Wikipedia. "Windows In Brighton Street, Edinburgh."
Wikipedia. 2023. https://commons.wiki-
media.org/wiki/File:Windows_in_Brighton_Street,_Edin-
burgh.jpg May 29, 2023.

# CHARRON MOCZYGEMBA